num pang

num pang

BOLD RECIPES FROM NEW YORK CITY'S
FAVORITE SANDWICH SHOP

Ratha Chaupoly & Ben Daitz

WITH RAQUEL PELZEL

Photographs by Ricky Powell | Art by Serve | Food Photographs by Evan Sung

Houghton Mifflin Harcourt
Boston · New York · 2016

For information about permission to reproduce selections from this book, write
to trade.permissions@hmco.com or to Permissions, Houghton Mifflin Harcourt
Publishing Company, 3 Park Avenue, 19th floor, New York, New York 10016.

www.hmhco.com

Library of Congress Cataloging-in-Publication Data
Names: Chaupoly, Ratha, author. | Daitz, Ben (Restaurateur), author.
Title: Num Pang : recipes from New York City's favorite sandwich shop /
    Ratha Chaupoly and Ben Daitz, with Raquel Pelzel ; Photographs by
    Ricky Powell ; Art by Serve ; Food Photographs by Evan Sung.
Description: Boston : Houghton Mifflin Harcourt, 2016. | Includes index.
Identifiers: LCCN 2015019993| ISBN 9780544534315 (paper over board) | ISBN
    9780544534940 (ebook)
Subjects: LCSH: Cooking, Cambodian. | Sandwiches—Cambodia. | Num Pang
    (Restaurant chain) | LCGFT: Cookbooks.
Classification: LCC TX724.5.C16 C49 2016 | DDC 641.59596—dc23
LC record available at http://lccn.loc.gov/2015019993

Printed in China
C&C 10 9 8 7 6 5 4 3 2 1

I would like to dedicate this to my dear mother—
our journey together has made me who I am. Your
love and support will always live in my heart.

—RATHA CHAUPOLY

This book is dedicated to the memories of my
father, Stephan Daitz, and my sister, Francesca
Daitz. Both were unique individuals and influenced
my life in more ways than can be counted.

—BEN DAITZ

acknowledgments

Ben and Ratha would like to thank their business partners Michael Nieberg, Dan Bartfeld, Richard Chapman, Randy Mcnamara, Patrick Milner, and Gordon Hamm. They would also like to thank their cookbook co-collaborators Raquel Pelzel, Evan Sung, Kira Corbin, Ricky Powell, Joe (Serve) Vega, and Laura Nolan, and their publicists Gita McCutcheon from Gita Group, and Phil Baltz, Ilana Alperstein, and Victoria Trinko from Baltz & Co., for putting up with them. In addition they would like to say a special thank-you to the numerous staffers that have been with them since the beginning.

FROM RATHA

I want to thank my son, Tristan, for always teaching me the way of life; to all my family and good friends who have propelled me to be a better man; and a special thank-you to the Howell Family: You guys rock.

FROM BEN

I would like to thank my mother, Mimi, and brother, Maurice, for their unconditional support. In addition, thanks to my inner circle (you know who you are) who have helped keep me on track in a variety of ways over the years. All of this would not have been possible without all of you.

FROM RAQUEL

From the time I met Ratha and Ben to the moment this book is published will have been three years, and over those years, each of our lives has changed in major and significant ways. I love you both so very much, and am thankful to not just have you in my life as collaborators but as trusted friends and confidants.

Thanks to my boys for always reminding me what's most important (baseball); to Evan Sung and Kira Corbin for making everything so gorgeous; to Ilana Alperstein for the introduction; to Stephanie Alleyne for your keen eye and assistance on recipes and at the shoot; to Brooks Halliday and Alexandra Utter for your testing prowess; to our agents Sarah Smith, David Black, and Laura Nolan for everything above and beyond; and to Justin Schwartz and the entire HMH team for believing in the power of Num Pang.

introduction

Not a pastrami on rye. Not a Reuben. Not an egg and cheese. It's a *num pang*, the Cambodian sandwich that is the specialty and namesake of our NYC-based restaurant chain, Num Pang. For three years running New Yorkers voted our version of the Vietnamese banh mi their go-to favorite sandwich. And it's no wonder—offering a taste of sweet, spicy, tangy, fresh, crunchy, and savory umami in every bite, a perfectly made *num pang* is a snapshot of contrasts, colors, and bold flavors. It's balanced, it's delicious, it's addictive.

A *num pang* offers all the elements of a meal in between two slabs of toasty semolina baguette: sweet-tart pickled carrots, fresh cucumber slices and cilantro, spicy chili mayo, and protein, be it fall-apart-tender ginger-braised brisket, soy-lacquered peppery catfish, or thick-cut bacon and greenmarket peaches.

Num Pang has a cult following for a reason—people just freak out for our cooking and the unique way we match pickles to proteins and complex sauces and glazes to herbs and spices. Our sandwiches, rice and noodle bowls, salads, and sides reflect flavor trends happening now: smoky-sweet, pickled, spicy, and umami all the way. The ingredients we use can be found in most every supermarket. In fact, the key sandwich component that tops *every single* Num Pang sandwich, the "Holy Trinity" (well, actually four ingredients—see page 39) is composed of pickled carrots, fresh cilantro and cucumber slices, and chili mayo. There's nothing hard to find or obscure about that. It just proves that there really isn't anything overly complicated about our food, even though it tastes exotic and bold. That's why our recipes are so home-cookable: most home cooks probably already have just about everything they need to make our fresh and modern dishes in their pantry.

We opened our first Num Pang in March 2009 in Union Square. That month we sold out of every sandwich, side, and soup, every single day. There were lines sixty-people deep waiting in sub-zero temperatures for our hoisin meatball *num pang* or five-spice-glazed pork belly *num pang*. It was nuts. It showed us that people are hungry for flavor, for something that tastes just exotic enough, yet touches on the familiar too. You probably won't find a pulled pork *num pang* or a skirt steak *num pang* in Cambodia, but you will find them at our shop and in our cookbook.

The Num Pang vibe is an important ingredient too—in every shop, we incorporate an intensely vivid urban feel, from the graffiti on the walls to the Golden Era hip-hop on the sound system and the general casualness of the space. The brightness in flavor is replicated in the brightness of the shops. They're modern, a little gritty, and totally transportive and accessible.

Almost immediately after we opened, we knew we had something. Which explains how we grew from one shop in 2009 to eight in 2015. That's no joke—it's the reason Grub Street called us New York City's "quietest restaurant empire." Today we have our flagship in the NoMad neighborhood, a small shop in Chelsea Market, a location near Times Square, one near Grand Central, one in the World Financial Center (at Brookfield Place's Hudson Eats), and our sleeker and better version across the street from the first Num Pang on 12th Street in the Village. With lots more to come.

MEET RATHA AND BEN. WE ARE NUM PANG.

We met in the mid-1990s at Clark University in Worcester, Massachusetts. Ben was studying political science, and Ratha, well . . . he showed up one day at a friend's house and never went home! Little did we know how important a chance and seemingly random meeting at a party (and probably over Jell-O shots) would be to our futures.

We liked each other from the start, and hung out with the same circles of friends, so we ended up in a lot of the same social situations and at the same parties. But when college was over, we did what kids do—we just went our separate ways. Ben went back to New York City and Ratha stayed in New England. It wasn't until a few years after college ended that we ran into each other again, just blocks from the future site of our first Num Pang location in New York City. Both of us, coincidentally, had landed in the food and hospitality business.

To look at us on paper, we're an odd couple. Ben grew up in NYC and was lucky enough to eat in a few of Europe's Michelin-starred restaurants; he also went to culinary school and has fine dining cooking chops. Ratha is a Cambodian refugee, grew up on three continents, dropped out of college, and is a totally self-taught cook. Yet here we are, running a thriving sandwich mini empire. Two friends from two totally different backgrounds, both feeding the American dream.

RATHA'S STORY: FROM CAMBODIA TO NYC

I was born in Phnom Penh, Cambodia. When I was six months old, the country fell to its knees and war took over everyone's lives. My father, a professor and high-ranking official in the Cambodian army, was taken away, leaving my mom to care for my two older brothers and me. She was barely twenty years old. We didn't hear from my father again until I was eighteen.

When I was two years old, we escaped Cambodia and found refuge in Vietnam, in an area near where my paternal grandparents lived in Takeo, Cambodia. My older brothers went to live with my grandparents, while I, the baby, stayed with Mom. We traveled around the country and sold medicine, walking to different villages, Mom arriving with her traveling luggage stocked with aspirin and other generic medicines, asking villagers if they needed anything. Along the way, we'd visit family members who had left Cambodia just like us.

We traveled around, eating typical Vietnamese dishes like *num pachok*, a noodle soup, or *banh xeo*, a rice flour crepe stained yellow from turmeric, filled with ground pork or chicken and loaded with scallions. We were vagabonds, and the one time my mom tried to settle someplace with some permanence, a small town where her sister lived, we had to leave two days after arriving because the Vietnamese army had surrounded the town and gunfire erupted. I was five years old and it was the first time I went to school, even if only for two days.

That was my gypsy life for many years. Vietnam was safer than Cambodia, but not safe in general, and Mom tried her best to get us out. She paid for passage on boats headed to Thailand twice, exorbitant fares both times. We'd sit on the boat for days with barely any water or food and no place to sleep. The boat would sail out onto the water, then turn around and return to Vietnam, really for no reason other than to take the passengers' money.

After that second failed attempt, my mom happened to run into a friend who suggested we check our status for the lottery to leave the country. In the late 1970s, you had to have your number called to get out of Vietnam. In a weird twist of fate, it just happened that while we were on the boat to nowhere, our luck came due, and Mom's number popped up—we would finally be allowed passage out of Vietnam.

My mom, my brothers, and I went to Austria for a year and then immigrated to the United States, to a small town on the Hudson River called Dobbs Ferry, one hour north of New York City. Other than that two-day failed stint at school in Vietnam when I was five, I hadn't been to school in four years, and I didn't know a lick of English. I remember that first day so vividly. The kids were studying math and the teacher called on me. I had never done math in my life except to help people pay for their medical supplies. Not only did I have no idea what the teacher was talking about, but I literally had no idea what she was saying. I sat there and stared straight ahead while the kids laughed at me. That was my first day.

After about a year, we moved to Connecticut, near the Hartford area. Mom worked her butt off, and on her days off, we'd hang out with other Cambodians. I remember this three-story apartment building that housed a bunch of other Cambodian families. I must have been eleven or twelve years old at the time. When we visited these friends, it was just a total feast. I mean, Mom could cook, and she cooked every day. But these women, man, they *cooked*. The way they seasoned their dishes and made them come alive, well, that was the moment when I fell hard for food and saw firsthand how food can bring people together and make them happy.

Believe it or not, I somehow graduated high school on time. I made a lot of wrong turns as a teenager, but eventually pulled my act together when, after visiting some friends at Clark University in Worcester, Massachusetts, I decided to transfer there, which turned out to be incredibly fortuitous, because that's where I met Ben.

When all my friends started graduating and moving away, I felt like I needed to do something else too. I moved to Lowell, Massachusetts, where I helped my brother with a sea urchin exporting business, and after a couple of years doing that, I took a job as a waiter at a Cambodian restaurant called Carambola in Waltham, Massachusetts. I was terrible at it at first, and honestly I think the only reason I got the job was because I was Cambodian. Even so, I fell into the work in a natural way—thinking on my feet was second nature. I worked my way up quickly and was promoted to management within six months, and then was transferred to the Elephant Walk, a French-Cambodian restaurant outside of Boston that was rapidly expanding. I helped them open a new location in Cambridge—it was an eye-opening experience for me, that the public would be interested in Cambodian food served in a fine-dining setting . . . even with wine! Wow, it was a totally new thing. I was there for a couple of years, then was ready to take on more responsibility and find a change of scenery. I wanted to learn more about wine and always had it in the back of my mind that I wanted to be in New York City, so I started looking for opportunities there. Then I heard about an opening at Blue Water Grill in New York City's Union Square, and I took it on the spot. After Blue Water and a few stints here and there in the city, I landed at Fleur de Sel, a boutique restaurant in Union Square, and worked with Chef Cyril Renaud. Being there afforded me the opportunity to learn more about wine—I built the list from one hundred to one thousand bottles. It was a family-oriented work environment where food and service were at the forefront of importance. It's really where I grew to love the restaurant business even more and came to think of my work not just as a job, but as my career and future.

BEN'S STORY:
A NEW YORK NATIVE SETS OUT FOR CAMBODIA

I'm a third-generation native New Yorker. I grew up on the Upper West Side near Columbia University. I was your normal city kid; I hung out with friends, listened to hip-hop, and got into my fair share of trouble. My parents were both academics—my mom was a professor of music, and my dad was a professor and chairman of a classical language department.

My dad, who was not an indulgent guy, splurged on two things: food and wine, and my mom brought me up to respect food and the sacred rituals of eating out. In fact, I had to pass a "manners" test at home before I was even allowed to go out to eat with them.

Since my parents were both total Francophiles (from the time I was born, my dad only spoke to me in French), I was reared on stinky French cheeses and sips of red wine, and every seven years when they each took sabbatical, we spent that time living in Paris. My parents clearly had their priorities in order, because when we traveled around Europe, we'd stay at the cheapest hotels and eat in Michelin-starred restaurants. I was eleven when I ate at Frédy Girardet's restaurant in Crissier, Switzerland. I remember sitting at the table after a meal created by someone considered to be the best chef *in the world*, trying to figure out the bright flavor in his elusive granita (I guessed it right: grapefruit), and then seeing Frédy slide into a gleaming gold Mercedes—the same model I'd seen in a bunch of hip-hop videos (my obsession)—and thinking, "Hey, it's pretty cool to be a chef!"

I didn't figure that being a chef might be in my future until after I graduated from Clark with my political science degree and absolutely no idea what the hell to do with it. So I started to think about what made me happiest. I knew for sure I didn't want to be an academic like my parents. While reflecting on what gave me the most satisfaction and contentment, I always came back to being around a table, to the gratification I received from food and the pleasure it gave me and my parents.

Now, this was the mid-1990s, just when chefs were starting to become names in the States, just when people were beginning to get more into food. Cooking school, a trade vocation, was not something my parents were keen for me to jump into lightly, so they arranged a meeting with a friend of theirs who was a chef in the French consulate in New York City. After talking to him, I decided to try out cooking life before committing to culinary school. I worked short stints at Daniel, Le Cirque, and Bouley. Standing for twelve hours in the kitchen, prepping, cooking, sweating, and stressing, sounds awful, but that feeling of total success at the end of the night—that euphoric post–dinner rush high—was incomparable to anything I had ever experienced. I was hooked.

I went to the Culinary Institute of America and in 1998 landed an externship at San Francisco's La Folie. I worked under Chef Roland Passot, pulling fourteen- and sixteen-hour shifts. Probably the most significant moment for me during that time, though, didn't happen in the kitchen but as a diner. One of my schoolmates was externing at The French Laundry with Thomas Keller. I drove to Yountville and experienced firsthand the magic of an eighteen-course meal prepared by Chef Keller—it was transcendent.

After my externship was over, I came home about thirty pounds thinner, and more committed than ever. Even though I was officially no longer attached to any university, I devised my own culinary "masters" program: I'd spend five years working in five of the best restaurants in New York City. I started under Floyd Cardoz at Tabla, which had just opened six months prior. Then I cooked with David Bouley at Danube. After so many years in fine dining, my next move was to Brooklyn's Rose Water, where I could slow things down a bit and learn more about greenmarket cooking. In 2001, I took a position as sous chef at the Michelin-starred restaurant Saul, where I cooked for two years.

Then I did something crazy: I left. I left the restaurant and I left cooking. I just needed a break from the lifestyle—the cooking and the physical intensity of it. A friend's uncle was a principal in a real estate firm and I started thinking about joining him. I ended up working with him and creating a restaurant-focused division, renting spaces and drafting leases for chefs.

Then I ran into Ratha, and, well, everything changed. Just when I thought I was out, he pulled me back in.

A PANG
IS BORN

We literally saw each other across a crowded room—in this case, the bar area at Blue Water Grill in New York City. Ben was working at Tabla, just a few blocks from Blue Water, and he came in for drinks with some friends. We saw each other—neither of us knew the other was living in New York City—and it was like no time had passed at all. Ben and a bunch of our friends became regulars at Blue Water—they'd hang out until closing and the whole gang would go out together afterward. We kind of kept up with each other in a loose way, you know, how you do in New York City. Ratha went to Tabla and asked for all kinds of weird substitutes and pairings, and Ben went to Blue Water to give Ratha a hard time. When Ben left the restaurant world to try his hand in real estate, it was just about the time that Ratha opened his very first restaurant, Kampuchea (Kamp for short) in 2006. This worked out well, as Ben was able to use his newfound "free time" to help Ratha open.

A hit with dining critics from the start, Ratha used Kamp to showcase the noodle and rice dishes that he grew up with as a Cambodian expat living in New England, as well as snacks and street foods. One of the most popular menu items was the *num pang* sandwich, an affordable and packed-with-flavor behemoth, essentially Cambodia's answer to Vietnam's banh mi.

Ratha wanted his *num pang*s to be as authentic as possible—little did he know the most trying component would be the bun. He played with countless recipes and tried hundreds of rolls, buns, and baguettes before he decided on *the one*. The baker he was working with, Frankie Parisi of Parisi's Bakery, definitely thought he was insane, and even kicked Ratha out of his bakery on more than one occasion. But Ratha knew that that the success of the *num pang* absolutely hinged on finding the most ideal combination of tender, soft interior with a crackling and crisp yet not-too-chewy crust. That recipe is, incidentally, nearly identical to the one we still use today.

Stuffed into that baguette was braised or grilled meats topped with a sweet-spicy sauce, spicy mayonnaise, pickled carrots, cucumbers, and cilantro. The whole package came together and *num pang*s were a runaway success. Ben found himself at Kamp all the time—the *num pang*s were his go-to menu item.

It didn't take long for the two of us to start thinking more seriously about *num pang* and the possibility of collaborating on an offshoot. Something young and cool, cheap and accessible; a fast-casual concept that capitalized on good technique and awesome flavor.

In late 2008, we found our location. We knew that a college audience—kids who wanted big flavors at cheap prices—would be a great fit for our sandwich shop, so we decided to hone in on the Union Square and New York University area. We both lived near this place at the corner of University and 12th Street. It had a car rental office on the ground floor and when the space came up for rent, we knew it would be perfect. It was 250 square feet on the ground floor and 250 square feet upstairs (about the size of a suburban bedroom)—just enough space to shoehorn in nine stools overlooking a garage.

We scraped together all the money we could. Savings, earnings, credit card cash advances. And in the spring of 2009, eight months after we had found the space and after renovating it on a total shoestring budget, we opened Num Pang.

Kampuchea was going strong and Ben had just found the space for the Vanderbilt, a gastropub-type spot in Brooklyn's up-and-coming Prospect Heights neighborhood. So we both had other things going on. But it didn't matter. From the moment we opened, we were both in the shop all the time.

We sold out every day for the first few months. Our kitchen footprint was *tiny*. We had a little oven and totally were unprepared for the sheer amounts of food we were going through every day. Lines were running forty to sixty people deep at all hours of the day! We just learned as we went along, and it didn't take long for us to figure out that in order for Num Pang to really be successful, we had to get more space. We turned a maintenance closet into a refrigerator. We took over the locksmith's space on the second floor, giving people a few tables and stools to sit at. We played cat and mouse with health inspectors since, well, only 75 percent of what we were doing, space-wise, was even legal! We were cooking, taking orders, expediting . . . we were there sixteen hours a day, seven days a week, for *months*.

Every sandwich was mindfully and intentionally created to present a perfect balance of flavors and textures. So when guests started making substitutions and special requests, it made us crazy—all that work to devise a specific experience was being lost. We had to find a way to exercise more control. Not that we were trying to be *num pang* police or anything, but we were working in such a fast-paced, high-volume setting that we had to create some parameters so our guests would enjoy the sandwiches as they were intended to be eaten. So, to ensure that everyone could find something on the menu, we took extra pains to create a menu that could accommodate everyone. We created a soy-based chili mayo and a chili-yogurt "mayo," as well as vegetarian *num pang*s and vegan salads and menu items just for eaters who had specific dietary needs.

It was also key to us not to allow the quality of food to suffer even though the volume was ever-increasing. So we came up with inside baseball lingo to keep the pressure of the line in check, like if we called out "86 pork!", it didn't mean we were out of pork. It meant "we are in the weeds, so slow it down!" Our kick-ass cashiers would know to stop taking orders, to spill something (or pretend to spill something) and take a minute to clean it up. That's the only way we could get a handle on it—we were two cooks, a dishwasher, and a cashier in this minuscule space. It was survival of the fittest!

Num Pang was so successful and only getting more and more recognition. We knew we had something there, something to build on. It was a perfect storm for us—banh mi sandwiches got really trendy, everyone's wallet was light due to the economic crash, and people wanted to eat well but were also conscious about what they were spending. It was a stroke of luck and really great timing.

In 2010, one year after the 12th Street shop opened, Kampuchea closed its doors. Which was all okay—because two years later we opened our second outpost of Num Pang at Grand Central in Midtown, and in 2013, we opened three new locations: our flagship in the NoMad neighborhood, a shop in Chelsea Market, and a location in Times Square. In 2014, we opened our Battery Park location and our new-and-improved 12th Street location in the Village; 2015 brought us to Manhattan's Financial District. We are busier than ever, and with several new locations on the way, there are no signs of us slowing down.

COOK. THIS. BOOK.

You think we sat down and spent two years (yes, people, two freaking years) working on this cookbook to have it sit in your house and collect dust? Um, no. You're going to cook from this book, and you're going to love it.

First, let it be said, this is not a cookbook of sandwiches, even though at its core, that's what Num Pang is all about. When we knocked our heads together to figure out how to capture the essence of our food, we figured that while we're crazy enough to spend a day marinating and upward of half a day braising a big hunk of meat for a sandwich, the average home cook might not be. That said, take the brisket (or the pork belly or chicken chimichurri, for that matter) off the sandwich, and you have an incredibly flavorful protein that can be the highlight of your dinner.

So we divided the book into chapters that made sense for us: Start Here is self-explanatory. It's the first place you should look for ideas. This is where the meaty recipes are (and, for fairness, the veggie and fish recipes too), the protein-heavy workhorses of a meal. It's a big chapter—nearly half the book. But this is the crux of our operation, the foundation of every *num pang*. And if, after roasting or braising or grilling that piece of meat, fish, or portobello mushroom, you have the desire to turn it (or the leftovers) into the best sandwich you'll ever put in your mouth, then we give you guidance on how to get there. At the tail end of every recipe in the Start Here chapter, you'll find instructions on how to "Num Pang It," or turn the recipe into a *num pang* (the only exception is when the recipe is actually for a *num pang* to start with—like the Num Pang Lobster Roll on page 123).

Pickles are a *huge* part of our food. We serve a pickle with just about everything, from sandwiches to noodle bowls, salads, and even to top lentil soup (page 173). That's why it's the second chapter: After deciding what main item you want to make from Start Here, you've got to go for a pickle component. Some are sweet, some are spicy, all are really easy. These are refrigerator pickles, not meant for preserving and patience but for people who want a pickle, like, now (or in an hour or two).

On the Side features items that we offer on the menu or not—these are just tasty tidbits like our glazed spicy chicken wings (page 162), Tamarind Baby Back Ribs (page 159), or our coconut and chili mayo topped grilled corn. In a Bowl: Hot, is where you'll find soups, stews, and warm bowl-friendly dishes like mussels with tomatillos and okra (page 191) and Oxtail Stew (page 183). In a Bowl: Cold, is the home to our chilled summer gazpacho (page 207), as well as salads and slaw (kale salad anyone?). Finally, our drinks have a whole chapter dedicated just to them. Addicted to our Cambodian Iced Coffee (page 222)? Now you can make it yourself.

With many of our recipes, we include a Heads-Up note—this relates a key bit of intel about the recipe that you should be keen on before diving in. If you have to marinate the meat overnight, or if you can substitute an easy-to-find ingredient for a more unusual one, you will probably find that information in the Heads-Up. We also wanted to explain certain ingredients, techniques, cuts, and ideas to readers in a more in-depth style, which is what you'll see in the Know This section. It's a source for the hows and whys behind what we do.

If you're looking to amp up your cooking game, turn the page, pick a recipe, and just go for it.

THE NUM PANG PANTRY

These are the ingredients you'll see popping up again and again in our recipes—they are the heart and soul of our cooking, and with them, you'll be prepared to make everything exactly how we do. Here's our list of pantry essentials.

ASIAN PEAR: Sweet and beautiful, what's not to love about this fruit? It's juicy like sugarcane, with a crispness that is reminiscent of daikon or jícama. It pickles nicely and is excellent alongside something fatty, heavy, or spicy.

DAIKON: Long and cylindrical, daikon is a generally mild radish that is very absorbent and crisp, making it a great vegetable to pickle and add crunch to *num pang*s. It takes on flavors nicely—think of it like the radish form of tofu. Even when it's cooked it holds its shape pretty well, though its crispness transforms to a meltingly tender texture.

DRIED SHRIMP AND FERMENTED SHRIMP PASTE: Dried shrimp are tiny thumbnail-size shell-on shrimp that are sun-dried or slowly oven baked. They are used whole or finely chopped into small bits and add an almost bacon-like meatiness to whatever they're stirred into. Fermented shrimp paste is made from dried, pulverized, salted, and fermented shrimp. It has an intense funk to it but smells a lot stronger than it tastes, especially since you always add just a small amount to a dish.

Preserved Whole Gouramy Fish In Bri
Salaison De Gourami En Entie

MẮM CÁ SẶC

NET WT : 15 oz (430 g)

OR :
RADING.
J6112.
TNAM

INGREDIENT
GOURAMY FISH, SUGA
RICE FLOUR, FISH
SODIUM BENZO

FISH SAUCE: Can we please put to rest the idea that fish sauce tastes fishy? This condiment has a deeply complex and unique flavor that is more salty-umami (think kimchi or kombucha) than fishy. It really has the power to boost the flavor of a dish to the next level—kind of like anchovy (another ingredient in need of a public relations overhaul) or miso paste. You're not going to want to sit at a table and do shots of it, but to not use it because you're afraid of its name is silly. Embrace the funk and let it move your food forward.

FIVE-SPICE POWDER: This spice blend has its origins in China, but is used in lots of Asian and Southeast Asian cuisines. It's typically made from five spices, including star anise, cloves, cinnamon, aniseed, and Sichuan peppercorns, though ingredients can be swapped depending on who is making it—for example, ginger sometimes stands in for the Sichuan pepper, fennel seed for the anise, and cardamom, orange peel, and even galangal can be incorporated. The assertive licorice-citrus flavor lends itself to pork. We use five-spice to cure pork belly (page 78) with maple syrup. While you can purchase it pre-blended, we advocate grinding your own (page 99) for the freshest, most intense taste.

FRIED ONIONS AND FRIED GARLIC: These are pretty crucial to many of our dishes. You can buy fried onions or garlic in large plastic tubs in Asian markets and they will last a long, long time in the pantry. We like how they add textural crunch as well as a base-level garlic or onion flavor as a garnish or finishing flavor, rather than in the beginning of the cooking process (as you'd use fresh onions or garlic). We use them a lot in salads and slaws—try them once and you'll be hooked too. If you can't find the premade stuff, you can deep-fry shallots and use them instead. See page 185 for directions.

GARLIC CHIVES: You can find these long chives in Asian markets. They kind of look like flat and long blades of grass and have a taste that is more garlicky than the oniony flavor of chives. If you can't find them, use regular chives and add a quarter to half of a minced garlic clove to get the garlic underpinning.

GINGER: Fresh ginger has a pretty amazing spicy, hot, and bright flavor. In Asian cooking, it is as important as garlic and onions. Young ginger has super-thin skin, and is slightly red tinted and less fibrous than more mature ginger. It also tastes milder and juicier, whereas older ginger packs more punch.

HOISIN SAUCE: We use the store-bought bottled stuff, and you should too. When choosing between brands, grab the one with the fewest additives. It's always nice to be able to recognize all the ingredients on a label for a product that is going to make it into your food and belly.

JASMINE RICE: Jasmine rice is a staple of Southeast Asian cooking. Most people think that jasmine and basmati rice are interchangeable, but they're so different. Jasmine is a shorter grain, more floral, and has a stickier texture than nutty basmati, which cooks up fluffier (it is used in Middle Eastern and Indian dishes). To put it simply: for Southeast Asians, it's not even a choice—it's jasmine all the way.

JASMINE TEA: Jasmine tea is wildly popular in Asia, and is made by infusing jasmine blossoms into green or black tea. We use the green tea in the stores; buy loose-leaf tea since it's usually of better quality and cheaper than the tea portioned into tea bags. (For more on jasmine tea, go to page 216.)

LEMONGRASS: Lemongrass is prized for its fresh, grassy, citrusy flavor. It tastes different than a lemon, making lemongrass well worth seeking out (most natural food markets and all Asian markets sell it). You can chop it, bash it, bruise it, and use it whole to add a lemony essence to sauces, marinades, soups, and stews. When choosing lemongrass, it should be bright and fragrant. If it looks dry and branchy, don't buy it. And definitely avoid bottled, dried lemongrass!

RICE VERMICELLI NOODLES: Made from rice (obviously), these thin, transparent dried noodles are cooked throughout Southeast Asia and are as much of a comfort food to Southeast Asians as spaghetti is to Italians. Some people soak them in water before cooking, but we just cut straight to the chase and boil them for a few minutes (almost more like blanching, really) before using. You can eat them hot or cold. Note that while cellophane noodles (also called glass noodles) look similar to rice vermicelli, they are made from a different starch (mung bean most commonly). In a pinch you can switch out one for the other, but they are not the same ingredient.

SAMBAL OELEK: This is really just garlic and dried chiles made into a kind of loose paste. There's not a lot of nuance to it straight up, but it makes an incredible base for glazes and sauces, especially when honey is involved to sweeten it and add body. Sambal oelek is easier to build on than Sriracha—you can always taste when Sriracha has been added to a dish, but if you add sambal it's harder to place and isn't quite as in-your-face.

SOY SAUCE: We think of soy sauce as more of a spice than a salt replacer. Even when we call for soy sauce, we'll still add salt to a dish. Soy sauce is yet another salty instrument to count on, and adds umami and complexity to marinades, sauces, or dressings.

SRIRACHA: Why wouldn't we like this stuff? Sriracha tastes a little more rounded and has a more garlicky flavor than the thinner, sweeter Sriracha equivalent found in Thailand and Cambodia. It's available pretty much everywhere and is probably on par with ketchup in popularity as a pantry condiment.

TAMARIND: The fruit of a brown pod, tamarind has a sweet-sour taste and is an important player in the food of Southeast Asia—it also happens to be the flavor base in Worcestershire sauce. It can be purchased in the pod (usually packed in a box) or the fruit can be compacted into a brick and then rehydrated (see the barbecue sauce on page 159), or you can buy it as a concentrate (we use the concentrate form in the tamarind–brown sugar drizzle on page 195 and in our Cambodian Iced Coffee, page 222). In a concentrate, tamarind is about the consistency of prune juice. We use the LA Lucky brand of *nuoc me chua* (tamarind concentrate), but there are lots of other brands readily available in Asian markets or online.

THAI BASIL: If we could bottle the essence of this alluring herb as a women's perfume, we would. With its peppery, star anise and licorice-y flavor, it is way more complex than Italian basil. Fresh Thai basil is readily available (and cheap!) in Asian and Indian markets, but if you can't find it, you can substitute Italian basil—just know that your dish will lose some dimension (sorry, but it's true). To extend the life of the basil, put the sprigs in a plastic bag with a wetted-and-squeezed-dry paper towel (and say a quick prayer to the basil gods). Though it's not a steadfast rule we follow all the time, generally speaking, we like using Thai basil as a finishing herb as opposed to a cooking herb since a lot of its nuance can be lost when exposed to heat.

THAI RED CHILES (FRESH AND DRIED): We use fresh and dried Thai bird's eye (red) chiles across the board in our food. These chiles are smaller, skinnier, and less astringent than the dried red cayenne chiles used whole, or more commonly, as red pepper flakes (the kind that comes in a shaker at pizza shops). Thai bird's eye chiles are spicy and bright and have a burn that doesn't sneak up on you. If you can't find fresh bird's eye chiles, substitute Fresno chiles (red jalapeños) or serrano chiles. Whole dried bird's eye chiles are pretty easy to find in Asian markets. To pulverize them into a finely textured flake, just pulse them in a spice grinder or food processor until the texture of the chiles is a bit finer than that of red pepper flakes. If you can't find them, substitute red pepper flakes.

UNSWEETENED DESICCATED COCONUT: When we use dried coconut flakes, we are *not* using that sweetened, shredded coconut you find in the baking aisle at the grocery store. The coconut we use (called desiccated coconut) has barely any moisture to it, and actually smells and tastes like coconut, not sugar. You can usually find it in stores like Whole Foods or in the organic aisle at the supermarket.

WHOLE CORIANDER SEEDS: Buy some whole coriander, pulverize it in a spice grinder (or even a coffee grinder), and you'll immediately be blown away by its fresh, lightly musky, grassy aroma. Another plus to grinding it yourself is that you control the texture—we like to keep it rough and somewhat flaky so it doesn't incinerate immediately on the grill. A rough grind also adds a nice textural quality to rubs and sauces.

KNOW THIS: SPICES

We can't stress enough how important it is to buy spices from a place that has a high turnover—you don't want your spices to have been sitting on some store's dusty shelves for a hundred years before buying them and bringing them home. There are loads of online sources for fresh spices, or search out a Middle Eastern or Asian market that sells spices in bulk for freshness (as well as at a good price).

Spices typically stay fresh—in their whole form—for up to one year, if stored in a cool, dark, and dry place; when ground, they'll stay fresh for about six months. We call for *lots* of spices in our food, so if you buy in bulk you can rest easy knowing you'll blow through your stash pretty quickly. Some of the spices we buy in whole form include cumin seeds, fennel seeds, black peppercorns, dried red chiles (see page 35), and mustard seeds.

THE HOLY TRINITY (OF FOUR)

On every *num pang*, you'll find these four components: fresh cucumber slices, fresh cilantro sprigs, chili mayo, and pickled carrots. This foursome is holy in our eyes. It adds a spicy, creamy, pickled, crunchy, juicy, and savory component to every sandwich and even some soups. Keep these items in your fridge and we can just about guarantee you'll find a million and one uses for them.

most important chili mayo

_____

Every great sandwich includes some kind of spread, and we'll say with authority that the tastiest one is mayonnaise. Add some sambal oelek (see The Num Pang Pantry, page 29), a spicy, garlicky chili sauce, and you have a mayo that is so good, it has near-addictive qualities—which is why it is a component of _every single Num Pang sandwich_. Whether the sambal is mixed with mayo or with vegan mayo or yogurt, the spicy, rich, and creamy dimension it adds to the sandwich helps balance the sweet tang of the pickles, the freshness of the cucumbers, and the robustness of the protein or vegetables. You can find sambal in the Asian foods aisle of most big supermarkets—and if you can't, a squirt of Sriracha is a fine substitute.

1 cup mayonnaise

2 tablespoons sambal oelek (see The Num Pang Pantry, page 29), plus more as needed

1½ teaspoons sugar

½ teaspoon kosher salt

½ teaspoon freshly ground black pepper

In a medium bowl, whisk together the mayonnaise, sambal, sugar, salt, and pepper. Taste and add more sambal if you want it spicier. Store in an airtight container in the refrigerator for up to 2 weeks.

VARIATION: CHILI-SOY MAYO Substitute vegan tofu mayonnaise for the mayonnaise in the Most Important Chili Mayo.

_____

VARIATION: CHILI YOGURT Substitute plain Greek yogurt for the mayonnaise, and substitute 1½ teaspoons honey for the sugar.

holy pickled carrots

———

We go through thousands of pounds of carrots every week. To say that pickled carrots are important to our sandwiches would be an understatement—they are key (see The Holy Trinity, page 39). A pickled component tops every Num Pang sandwich and more often than not, that pickle is shredded and pickled carrots. Our carrots lean more to the sour side than to sweet or salty, and the kind of apple cider vinegar you use can greatly impact their flavor. Generally speaking, we've found that cheaper, harsher apple cider vinegar needs a little extra water, sugar, and sometimes a little extra salt mixed in to the pickle to soften its flavor. Higher-end apple cider vinegar often has a rounder and less abrasive flavor.

1½ cups sugar, plus more as needed

1¼ cups apple cider vinegar

1 cup distilled white vinegar

2 tablespoons kosher salt, plus more as needed

4 large carrots, grated (about 4 cups)

1   In a large bowl, whisk together the sugar, vinegars, and salt until the sugar and salt have dissolved. Add the carrots and stir to combine.

2   Let the carrots sit in the vinegar brine for at least 20 minutes before using. Taste them—they should be balanced, not very salty, and slightly more sour than sweet. If the flavor needs to be adjusted, add a little more sugar, salt, or a splash of water to lessen the intensity of the vinegar. Transfer the carrots and brine to an airtight container and refrigerate for up to 2 weeks.

heads-up

Sub in rice vinegar for the apple cider vinegar for an even subtler taste.

KNOW THIS: A FEW WORDS ON CUCUMBERS AND CILANTRO

In their unadulterated forms, cucumber and cilantro provide two different things. The cilantro is all about power and freshness. There is no denying that its herbaceous quality comes through loud and proud. The cucumber, on the other hand, is more about its cold, fresh snap than its flavor, which is quite muted and mellow, especially with the high-octane players (chili mayo and pickled carrots). Both are critical to the interplay of hot/spicy/crunchy/creamy/cold/warm/fresh/cooked and so on and so forth. We like to leave the cilantro leaves attached to the tender stems—those stems add even more concentrated flavor in a slightly different textural bite. The cucumber, we like to slice into long planks lengthwise and lay on the baguette, about two planks per sandwich. This allows the cucumber to become a consistent layer, offering its contributions in every bite.

KNOW THIS: THE PERFECT BREAD

We considered sharing the recipe in this book, but hey, we can't give away *all* our secrets! So we'll share a vital tip for making whatever bun you choose to use that much better: toasting it. Toasting the baguette warms it up just enough to re-crisp the exterior and soften the interior. Toast it cut-side down on a grill or cut-side up under a broiler to get that tinge of bitter that comes from the flame hitting the crumb. Toasting the bread brings extra complexity to our sandwiches, not just in the texture and crackle of the bun, but in the way the warmth of the baguette interacts with the chill of the cucumber and cilantro.

THE NUM PANG.

In Cambodia, at any meal at any time of day, you sit down to a table packed from end to end with different dishes. Pickles, roasted and braised meats, soups, relishes, hot sauces, raw vegetable salads, cooked vegetables, rice, and noodles . . . you name it. Hands are reaching across the table grabbing this, passing that, and the scene is slightly chaotic and generally full of energy and of course the excitement of a great meal. On a *num pang*, we try to pack that energy and those flavors into a baguette rather than spread them out over a table. A sandwich is basically the ultimate blank canvas that can be sketched in with a wide variety of flavor and textures. Contrasts happen in every bite. They are what makes our sandwiches unique and ultimately satisfying from first bite to last.

a num pang illustrated

BAGUETTE TOP

PICKLED CARROTS

CILANTRO

CUCUMBER SLICES

PROTEIN/VEG

CHILI MAYO

BAGUETTE BOTTOM

PART ONE

start here

WE TREAT SANDWICHES the same way that a chef might approach a plated composition: offer a distinct interplay between richness and acidity, temperature, tenderness and crunch, and raw and cooked. That's why each of our *num pang*s includes a pickle (or two), a spicy mayo, fresh herbs, and fresh cucumber slices. Once you peel away those components, however, you're left with what we like to think of as the heart of the sandwich: the protein (or vegetable). That's what we show you how to make in this chapter: thirty-eight ways to build a great-tasting meal. The protein or vegetable component is the foundation we start with when building a *num pang*, but really, it's the entry point to a satisfying meal. In this chapter you'll find recipes for Hoisin Meatballs (page 95) and roasted cauliflower (page 128), Seared Coconut Tiger Shrimp (page 117) and fried chicken (page 50). These bases are the foundation of our *num pang*s. Whether you choose to put it all on a baguette is your decision to make (and if you choose to go that route, check out Num Pang It at the end of the recipe). We highly recommend serving any of these proteins and vegetable-centric dishes with a pickle (or two)—there are plenty to choose from on pages 134 to 144.

CHICKEN, TURKEY & DUCK

ROAST CHICKEN CHIMI 49

CHILE-BASIL FRIED CHICKEN 50

DAN KLUGER'S CHICKEN SALAD WITH CASHEW
   BUTTER AND CRISPY CHICKEN SKIN 52

CHICKEN LIVER PÂTÉ WITH CORNICHONS 54

GLAZED FIG AND CRISPY CHICKEN SKIN NUM PANG 57

HONEY-BRINED ROAST TURKEY BREAST WITH
   CRANBERRY-APPLE CHUTNEY 60

FLOYD CARDOZ'S BLACK PEPPER CHICKEN 62

CHILE-RUBBED TURKEY WITH
   CELLOPHANE NOODLE STUFFING 63

CRISPY-SKIN DUCK BREAST WITH
   BLACK PLUM CHUTNEY 67

MICHAEL ANTHONY'S EPIC DUCK MEAT LOAF 69

roast chicken chimi

Argentine chimichurri sauce is a bright, herby, and acidic sauce that can be easily adapted to have a Southeast Asian slant. We add fresh ginger and substitute Thai basil for parsley, and there you have it—Num Pang's take on chimichurri. Chicken thighs are way more succulent than chicken breasts. They are easier to work with too—since they don't dry out as easily as chicken breasts, there is more margin for error, and you don't have to be super worried about overcooking them.

CHICKEN

2 cups canola oil

½ cup fresh lemon juice (from 2 to 3 lemons)

10 garlic cloves, coarsely chopped

Heaping 3 tablespoons coarsely chopped peeled fresh ginger

1½ cups fresh Thai or Italian basil leaves

½ cup fresh cilantro leaves

2 tablespoons kosher salt

1 tablespoon freshly ground black pepper

3 pounds boneless, skinless chicken thighs

CHIMI SAUCE

1 cup canola oil

1 cup apple cider vinegar

1 small jalapeño

5 garlic cloves, coarsely chopped

1 cup fresh Thai or Italian basil leaves

1 cup fresh cilantro leaves

Heaping ¼ cup coarsely chopped peeled fresh ginger

2 tablespoons kosher salt

2 teaspoons freshly ground black pepper

2 teaspoons yellow mustard seeds

¼ teaspoon sugar

1   **MARINATE THE CHICKEN:** In a blender, combine the oil, lemon juice, garlic, basil, cilantro, ginger, salt, and pepper in that order. Blend until the mixture is mostly smooth. Place the chicken thighs in a large airtight container and cover with the marinade. Cover the container and refrigerate for at least 12 hours or up to 24 hours.

2   **MAKE THE CHIMI SAUCE:** In a blender, combine the oil, vinegar, jalapeño, ginger, garlic, basil, cilantro, salt, pepper, mustard seeds, and sugar. Blend until pretty smooth. Pour 1 cup of the chimi sauce into a small bowl for basting and set the rest aside for serving.

3   Preheat the oven to 500°F. Line a baking sheet with aluminum foil.

4   Remove the chicken from the marinade and place it on the lined baking sheet. Roast the chicken for 10 minutes, then begin basting it occasionally with some of the chimi sauce until the chicken is browned and cooked through, 20 to 25 minutes more. Serve the chicken with the reserved chimi sauce on the side (discard any sauce leftover from basting).

heads-up

The chicken needs to marinate overnight for the best flavor. If you're tight on time, 6 hours will do.

num pang it

Holy Trinity (page 39), toasted bun

chile-basil fried chicken

Take a classic buttermilk brine, spike it with chile salt (see Know This, page 51) and Thai basil, roll that brined chicken around in self-rising flour, and you get the best fried chicken. Seriously. The acid in the buttermilk reacts with the leaveners in the flour (baking powder and baking soda) so that while the chicken fries, the breading puffs and crackles in craggy peaks, giving you everything you want in a fried chicken coating: crunchy, caramelized perfection. We fry boneless, skinless breasts since they lend themselves nicely to building a *num pang*. This method totally works with bone-in, skin-on chicken too—just increase the cooking time a bit to account for the bigger pieces of chicken.

CHILE SALT

5 dried Thai bird's eye chiles, or 1½ teaspoons red pepper flakes

¼ cup kosher salt

FRIED CHICKEN

3 cups buttermilk

½ cup slivered fresh Thai or Italian basil leaves

4 large boneless, skinless chicken breasts, halved lengthwise (so you have 8 thin pieces), or 8 chicken cutlets

Canola oil, for frying (6 to 8 cups, depending on your pot)

2 cups self-rising flour

1 lime, cut into wedges

1 **MAKE THE CHILE SALT:** Place the chiles in a small skillet and dry toast over medium-high heat until they are slightly puffed and fragrant, 20 to 30 seconds on each side (if using red pepper flakes, skip this step). Coarsely chop the chiles and place them in a mortar with the salt, then use a pestle to pulverize the mixture. (You can also pulse the mixture a mini food processor or coffee/spice grinder, though this will yield a finer-textured salt unless you pulse the chiles with half of the salt to start, then stir in the remaining salt to finish.)

2 **BRINE THE CHICKEN:** Mix the buttermilk, basil, and 1½ tablespoons of the chile salt together in an airtight container (or gallon-size resealable plastic bag). Add the chicken breasts and turn to coat. Cover the container and refrigerate overnight.

3 Fill a large heavy-bottomed pot with oil to a depth of 3 inches. Heat the oil over medium-high heat until it registers 350°F to 365°F on an instant-read thermometer.

4 While the oil heats, put the flour in a large bowl. Remove a piece of chicken from the brine. Fish out some of the basil and pat it on top of the chicken. Place the chicken in the flour and use your fingers to sprinkle a generous amount of flour over the top of the chicken so it is thoroughly coated. Remove the chicken from the flour and place it on a plate. Repeat with the remaining pieces of chicken.

KNOW THIS: MAKE
SEASONED CHILE SALT

Introduce an ingredient to coarse salt, apply friction, and you get a seasoned salt that rises way above either of its individual components. To season our fried chicken, we makes a chile salt by grinding toasted, dried red chiles into kosher salt, releasing the chiles' essential oils and giving a subtle heat to the salt. A rough-textured mortar and pestle does the job best, but a mini food processor, spice grinder, or coffee mill gets the job done too. Something about how the chile interacts with the salt gives the chile salt this umami-savory quality. Keep a bowl of it on your table and watch how quickly it disappears (it's great on fruit too).

5   Set a wire rack over a rimmed baking sheet and set aside. Add the breaded chicken to the oil one piece at a time. You may only have enough space to fry two or three pieces of chicken at a time (don't overcrowd the pan or the chicken may stick together and the temperature of the oil will drop too much, yielding greasy chicken). Fry, using a slotted spoon or chopsticks to turn the chicken occasionally, until both sides are golden-brown, the breading is crisp, and the chicken is cooked through, 7 to 8 minutes (decrease or increase the heat under the oil as needed to maintain an oil temperature around 360°F). Transfer the fried chicken to the rack and, while still hot, sprinkle with more of the chile salt. Repeat with the remaining pieces of chicken.

6   Serve with lime wedges.

heads-up

This recipe involves overnight brining and deep frying. As the basil fries, the essential oils are released and add lots of flavor to the fried chicken. That's what makes it so killer.

num pang it

Holy Trinity (page 39), Cambodian Slaw (page 198), toasted bun

dan kluger's chicken salad
with cashew butter and crispy chicken skin

———

Ben cooked alongside Dan Kluger, the former chef of ABC Kitchen in Manhattan (a stone's throw from the original 12th Street Num Pang location), in the late 1990s at Tabla in Manhattan, and the two have been good friends ever since. Dan came up with this incredibly nuanced and insanely good take on chicken salad for his ABC Pang, one of many sandwiches created for our Guest Chef charity program (see page 59). It's rich from the cashew butter and crunchy from cashew halves and pickled jalapeños, and has tons of freshness and acidity from citrus zest, citrus juice, and candied ginger. Half of the proceeds from every sandwich sold went to a charity Dan supports, the Edible Schoolyard program, which partners with New York City public schools in low-income neighborhoods to introduce kids to the concept of sustainability and help create and maintain on-site gardens; the other half of the proceeds went to our charity of choice, the Double H Ranch, a camp in upstate New York that offers support, recreation, and therapeutic experiences to children with life-threatening illnesses.

PICKLED RADISHES AND JALAPEÑOS

6 medium radishes, finely chopped

2 small jalapeños, thinly sliced

1 to 1¼ cups champagne vinegar

POACHED CHICKEN

1 (4-pound) chicken

Heaping 1 cup fresh Thai or Italian basil
 leaves, torn

Heaping ½ cup coarsely chopped
 peeled fresh ginger

4 garlic cloves, smashed

2 pieces kombu seaweed (½ ounce),
 broken into small pieces

1 fennel bulb, stalks and fronds
 removed (reserve for another use),
 bulb halved, cored, and coarsely
 chopped

Heaping ½ cup kosher salt

1   **PICKLE THE RADISHES AND JALAPEÑOS:** Combine the radishes and jalapeños in an airtight container and pour enough of the vinegar over them until they are just covered. Cover the container and set aside.

2   **POACH THE CHICKEN:** Remove the legs from the chicken, dividing each into a drumstick and a thigh. Slice through the breastbone to yield 2 chicken breasts (save the carcass and wings to make stock another time). In a Dutch oven or large pot, combine 12 cups water, the basil, ginger, garlic, kombu, fennel, and salt. Bring the mixture to a boil, turn off the heat, and let it cool for 30 minutes. Add the chicken pieces to the pot, cover, and return to a simmer over medium heat. Gently simmer (reduce the heat to medium-low if needed) for 15 minutes, then turn off the heat and let the chicken rest for 30 minutes. Remove the chicken from the poaching liquid and set aside. Discard the poaching liquid.

3   Preheat the oven to 325°F. Line a rimmed baking sheet with parchment paper.

CHICKEN SALAD

1¼ cups Most Important Chili Mayo (page 40)

½ cup coarsely chopped fresh Thai or Italian basil leaves

Grated zest of ½ lime

2 tablespoons lime juice (from about 1 lime)

1 tablespoon kosher salt

¼ cup cashew halves

CASHEW BUTTER

2 cups whole unsalted roasted cashews

¼ cup crystallized ginger

Grated zest of 4 lemons

2 fresh Thai bird's eye chiles, halved lengthwise

2 tablespoons kosher salt

2 tablespoons canola oil

SANDWICH

4 baguettes, split lengthwise and toasted

1 medium Kirby cucumber, thinly sliced lengthwise on an angle into 6 long planks

1 cup cherry tomatoes, halved

Holy Pickled Carrots (page 42)

12 fresh cilantro sprigs

4 Carefully remove and save the skin from the chicken breasts, thighs, and drumsticks and wipe off any residue from the poaching liquid and any extra fat. Lay the skin flat on the lined baking sheet and bake until it is browned and crisp, 20 to 30 minutes. Transfer the chicken skin to a paper towel–lined plate to drain and cool. Meanwhile, remove the meat from the drumsticks and thighs and finely shred it; remove the breast meat from the bones and chop it into very small pieces.

5 **MAKE THE CHICKEN SALAD:** Drain the pickled radishes and jalapeños in a fine-mesh sieve and transfer them to a large bowl. Stir in the chili mayo, basil, lime zest, lime juice, salt, and cashews, then add the chicken and stir to combine.

6 **MAKE THE CASHEW BUTTER:** In a food processor, combine the cashews, ginger, lemon zest, chiles, salt, oil, and ½ cup water and process until completely smooth. If the mixture is very stiff and thick, add up to 3 tablespoons more water, 1 tablespoon at a time, until it is spreadable.

7 **ASSEMBLE THE SANDWICH:** Spread a thin layer of cashew butter on both sides of each baguette. Add a few cucumber slices to the bottom baguette half and top with chicken salad, then follow with a few tomato halves, pickled carrots, and cilantro sprigs. Divide the crispy chicken skin over the carrots and place the other baguette half on top. Serve.

chicken liver pâté with cornichons

After Ratha moved to the States from Cambodia, his mother connected with other Cambodian women who collectively cooked and cared for one another's children when the moms were working. This pâté isn't some traditional Cambodian dish, but is something Ratha grew up eating, prepared by his extended family of Cambodian "aunties." A little sugar added with the salt and pepper helps the gizzards and hearts caramelize and brings up the base flavor, as does a splash of Guinness added at the end. The gizzards add texture and chew to the pâté—if you prefer a creamier spread, leave them out and substitute an equal amount of liver.

½ cup plus 2 teaspoons canola oil

1 medium yellow onion, coarsely chopped

6 lemongrass stalks, tough outer layer removed, tender inner reed thinly sliced on an angle

4 garlic cloves, finely chopped

1 (2-inch) piece fresh ginger, halved lengthwise and smashed

3 teaspoons coarse cane sugar or granulated sugar

2½ teaspoons kosher salt

½ teaspoon freshly ground black pepper, plus more for serving

16 chicken gizzards, trimmed of fat and chopped

16 chicken hearts

2 pounds chicken livers

1 cup Guinness beer

2 teaspoons apple cider vinegar

4 tablespoons (2 ounces) unsalted butter, at room temperature

16 cornichons, thinly sliced, plus more for serving

Toasted bread or crackers, for serving

1   In a large skillet, heat ½ cup of the oil over medium-high heat. Add the onion, reduce the heat to medium, and cook, stirring occasionally, until the onion softens and starts to color around the edges, 6 to 8 minutes. Stir in the lemongrass, garlic, ginger, 2 teaspoons of the sugar, 1½ teaspoons of the salt, and the pepper and cook, stirring often, until the lemongrass browns around the edges, 2 to 3 minutes.

2   Stir in the gizzards and hearts and cook, stirring occasionally, until they are cooked all the way through, about 15 minutes.

3   Increase the heat to high and stir in the chicken livers, remaining 1 teaspoon salt, and remaining 1 teaspoon sugar. Reduce the heat to medium-high and cook, stirring occasionally, until the livers are cooked through, about 20 minutes.

4   Once the chicken livers are cooked through, pour in the Guinness and continue to cook until small dots of oil separate and rise to the top of the sauce, about 10 minutes. Turn off the heat and set aside to cool completely, then remove and discard the ginger.

recipe continues

heads-up

The pâté takes at least 12 hours to firm up in the fridge before it's ready to serve.

num pang it

Holy Trinity (page 39), toasted baguette

5   Line a 1½-quart terrine mold (or 9 by 5-inch loaf pan) with plastic wrap. When the chicken liver mixture has cooled, transfer it to a blender, add the vinegar and remaining 2 teaspoons oil, and blend until smooth. Add the butter and blend until it is worked in. Scrape the chicken liver mixture into a medium bowl, fold in the sliced cornichons, then turn the mixture out into the prepared mold. Use a rubber spatula to press the mixture into the sides and corners of the container. Cover the top flush with plastic wrap and refrigerate overnight or for up to 3 days.

6   The next day, remove the plastic wrap from the top of the pâté and turn it out onto a serving platter. Remove the plastic wrap from the pâté and grind a few twists of black pepper over the top before serving with toasted bread or crackers and more cornichons on the side.

KNOW THIS: TOUGH LEMONGRASS LOVE

Trying to eat the tough outer layer of a lemongrass stalk is like trying to chew through tree bark. Sure, it's possible, but do you really want to go there? Well . . . kind of. The outer thick and fibrous paper covering of lemongrass has lots of lemongrass flavor, so instead of throwing it away, knot it and stash it in the fridge (it will keep for a week or so), then add it to soup, a sauce, or even herbal tea to infuse the liquid with lemongrass flavor. Cool, right?

glazed fig and crispy chicken skin num pang

One of our personal favorites as well as most popular *num pang*s is the glazed peach and bacon (page 82). It's that combination of sweet heat, fatty crunch, smoke, and juiciness that is like total sandwich nirvana. We tap into the same pleasure zone in this combination: spicy soy-glazed juicy-ripe figs and salty-crackly fried chicken skin. Now there is no way we could ever make this sandwich to feed the thousands upon thousands of hungry New Yorkers who stream into our shops every day. But at home, it's totally do-able. Of course you can swap bacon for the chicken skin, but you'll be missing out—the chicken skin is like crispy porky lace compared to a more solid plank of bacon.

CHICKEN SKIN

4 skin-on chicken breasts, skin removed (save the meat for another time)

½ teaspoon kosher salt

GLAZED FIGS

2 tablespoons apple cider vinegar

¼ teaspoon honey

¼ teaspoon soy sauce

¼ teaspoon ground dried Thai bird's eye chile, plus a pinch

¼ teaspoon kosher salt, plus a pinch

10 fresh black Mission figs, halved lengthwise

NUM PANG

1 tablespoon canola oil

1 medium jalapeño, thinly sliced on an angle into rounds

2 scallions, trimmed and cut into 1-inch segments

¼ teaspoon kosher salt

Freshly ground black pepper

2 (6-inch) baguettes, split lengthwise and toasted

3 tablespoons Most Important Chili Mayo (page 40)

1 medium Kirby cucumber, thinly sliced lengthwise on an angle into 6 long planks

8 sprigs fresh cilantro

⅔ cup Holy Pickled Carrots (page 42)

1   **MAKE THE CHICKEN SKIN:** Heat a medium skillet over low heat. Sprinkle both sides of the chicken skin with the salt and place the skin in the pan. Cook the skin, using a spatula to press it down firmly, until it starts to brown, about 1 minute, then flip the skin over and brown on the other side, pressing down firmly, about 1 minute more. Continue to cook, flipping the skin occasionally, until both sides are deeply browned, 15 to 20 minutes more. Transfer the crispy skins to a paper towel–lined plate to drain.

2   **MAKE THE GLAZED FIGS:** Preheat the oven to 450°F. Line a rimmed baking sheet with aluminum foil.

3   In a small bowl, mix together the vinegar, honey, soy sauce, a pinch of dried chile, and a pinch of salt. Set the figs, cut-side up, on the lined baking sheet, season with the remaining ¼ teaspoon dried chile and ¼ teaspoon salt, then drizzle with the vinegar mixture. Bake the figs until the glaze is bubbling and the cut sides of the figs burst a bit in the center, 7 to 8 minutes. Remove from the oven and set aside.

4   **MAKE THE NUM PANG:** Heat the oil in a small skillet over medium-high heat. Add the jalapeño, scallions, salt, and some black pepper, reduce the heat to medium, and cook, stirring often, until the jalapeño is tender, 3 to 4 minutes. Transfer the jalapeño and scallions to the plate with the chicken skins.

recipe continues

So yeah, you're totally going to peel away the chicken skin from the breast and save the breast meat for another time. It might sound weird to just use the chicken skin, but think of how good it's going to taste! Most butchers will sell you chicken skin, so call, ask, and make your life easier.

5   Spread both sides of each baguette half with the chili mayo. On the bottom bun half, add half the glazed figs and top with half the jalapeño-scallion mixture. Lay a few pieces of the crispy chicken skin on top. On the other bun half, add the cucumber slices followed by the cilantro and the pickled carrots. Press the two halves together and repeat for the other sandwich.

KNOW THIS: PAY IT FORWARD

Part of being successful business owners, restaurateurs, and good humans is giving back, helping those in need, and supporting worthy causes. We've raised over one hundred thousand dollars for charity over the years. In addition to our work as a company supporting organizations like the Food Bank for New York City and sending financial relief to help victims of Haiti's earthquake, we created the Guest Chef program, through which we can partner with chef friends of ours on a *num pang* collaboration that benefits a charity of the chef's choice. The profits from every sandwich sold are split equally between the chef's selected charity and ours. Check out the incredible sandwiches created by chefs and friends including Dan Kluger (page 52), Floyd Cardoz (page 62), Michael Anthony (page 69), Mario Batali (page 86), and Ad-Rock (page 96). Here are the charities we choose to support; see page 227 for contact information if you would like to make a contribution—be it a financial one, or a contribution of your time as a volunteer.

BARC (Brooklyn Animal Resource Coalition)

Cambodian Children's Fund

Double H Ranch

Edible Schoolyard NYC

Food Bank for New York City

God's Love We Deliver

The Young Scientist's Foundation

North Shore Animal League

Tuesday's Children

honey-brined roast turkey breast with cranberry-apple chutney

We all know the best part of Thanksgiving is the day-after turkey sandwich, right? Our turkey *num pang* was created with that in mind. We created it to tap into the flavors and textures we like to play off in all our sandwiches: sweet and tangy, spicy and pickled, creamy and crunchy—while also reminding us of turkey day. Here, we backpedal the recipe to its essence: a great brined and roasted turkey for the most flavorful and moist meat, and an excellent cranberry chutney that puts the canned stuff to shame. If you prefer, you can use maple syrup in place of the honey. And it goes without saying (but we're saying it anyway) to save leftovers for sandwiches the next day.

HONEY-BRINED TURKEY

1 gallon hot water

3 cups kosher salt

1¼ cups honey

¾ cup sugar

½ cup whole coriander seeds

5 tablespoons whole black peppercorns

3 dried bay leaves

8 cups ice cubes

1 (6- to 7-pound) whole bone-in, skin-on turkey breast

Canola oil, for greasing the roasting rack

CRANBERRY-APPLE CHUTNEY

12 whole star anise

1 tablespoon canola oil

2 tablespoons finely chopped peeled fresh ginger

5 cups dried cranberries

1 red apple, such as a McIntosh, peeled, cored, and chopped into ½-inch pieces

4 cups apple cider

½ cup sugar

1 tablespoon kosher salt

1 cup apple cider vinegar

1   **BRINE THE TURKEY:** In a large plastic tub, whisk together the hot water, salt, honey, and sugar until the salt and sugar have dissolved. Add the coriander, peppercorns, and bay leaves. Add the ice cubes and, once the brine is cool (you may need to refrigerate it for 1 to 2 hours to cool it down), add the turkey breast. Cover and refrigerate overnight.

2   **ROAST THE TURKEY:** Remove the turkey from the brine. Rinse thoroughly with cold water and pat dry with paper towels. Let the breast sit out at room temperature for 1 hour.

3   Preheat the oven to 450°F. Set a roasting rack in a roasting pan. Lightly oil the rack, then place the turkey on the rack, breast-side up. Roast until the turkey skin is golden, about 20 minutes. Reduce the oven temperature to 325°F and roast until the temperature in the thickest part of the breast reads 155°F on an instant-read thermometer, about 1 hour and 20 minutes longer.

A bone-in turkey breast is our choice for the best flavor and moistest meat, but if all you can find is boneless turkey breast, that works too—just keep an eye on the thermometer as it might cook more quickly than the bone-in breast.

num pang it

Heat the turkey slices in warm chicken stock or broth; while warm, add to a toasted baguette with Cranberry-Apple Chutney and Holy Trinity (page 39).

4 **MAKE THE CRANBERRY-APPLE CHUTNEY:** Place the star anise in a spice grinder and pulverize. Measure out ¾ teaspoon and save the rest for another time. In a large saucepan, heat the oil and the ground star anise over medium heat, stirring often, until fragrant and toasted, 1 to 2 minutes, then stir in the ginger and cook until fragrant, 1 to 2 minutes. Add the cranberries, apple, apple cider, and 4 cups water. Stir in the sugar and salt and bring the mixture to a simmer over high heat, stirring often to dissolve the sugar. Reduce the heat to medium-low and simmer, stirring occasionally, until the cranberries are very soft, the apples are falling apart, and the liquid has reduced by about half, about 15 minutes.

5 Fill a blender two-thirds full with the cranberry mixture. Add 2 tablespoons of the vinegar and puree, tasting and adding more vinegar as needed (you want the predominate flavors to be cranberry, ginger, and star anise with the vinegar acting to add balance rather than acidity). Transfer the mixture to a serving dish and repeat with the rest of the cranberry mixture and vinegar, working in batches and adding as much vinegar as is needed to create a well-balanced chutney.

6 Remove the roasting pan from the oven and transfer the turkey breast to a carving board. Loosely tent with aluminum foil and let the turkey rest for 10 minutes before slicing the breast meat off the bone into thin pieces. Serve with the cranberry chutney on the side.

floyd cardoz's black pepper chicken

serves 4

Floyd Cardoz, the chef of The Bombay Canteen in Mumbai and formerly the chef of White Street, North End Grill and Tabla in Manhattan, gave Ben his very first kitchen job at Tabla. Here, he shares a version of a recipe that he created for our Guest Chef program (see page 59 for more details). Half of the charitable contributions raised through sales of his Cardoz Pang went to The Young Scientists Foundation, a program that connects high school–age kids with bona fide scientists to mentor them throughout various stages of scientific research. The other half of the donation on Num Pang's behalf went to Tuesday's Children, which offers support and programming for children affected by 9/11.

3 medium garlic cloves, coarsely chopped

2 tablespoons ground coriander (preferably freshly ground; see page 122)

1½ tablespoons freshly ground black pepper

Heaping 1 tablespoon coarsely chopped peeled fresh ginger

⅛ teaspoon ground cardamom

⅛ teaspoon ground cloves

1 tablespoon canola oil

2½ pounds bone-in, skin-on chicken thighs

1½ teaspoons kosher salt

1 cup full-fat plain yogurt

num pang it

Add the thigh meat to the sauce; toss to combine. Add a large pinch of chopped fresh mint to Chili Yogurt (page 40), then spread on a toasted baguette. Add some chicken, sauce, a few coarsely chopped mint leaves, and Holy Trinity (page 39).

1   Preheat the oven to 325°F.

2   In a food processor, combine the garlic, coriander, pepper, ginger, cardamom, cloves, and 2 tablespoons water and process into a paste.

3   In a large oven-safe skillet, heat the oil over medium-high heat until it shimmers, about 2 minutes. Season the chicken with salt, then add the chicken to the pan, skin-side down, and cook until browned, about 8 minutes. Turn the chicken over and brown the other side, cooking until the moisture in the pan evaporates, about 5 minutes more (the chicken will finish cooking later). Transfer the chicken to a large plate and set aside.

4   Reduce the heat to medium-low and add the spice paste to the pan. Cook, stirring with a wooden spoon to scrape up any browned bits from the bottom of the pan, until the garlic is fragrant, about 2 minutes. Stir the yogurt into the spice paste, then return the chicken to the pan, skin-side up. Place the pan in the oven and braise until the chicken is cooked through and no longer pink near the bone, 35 to 40 minutes.

5   Remove the skillet from the oven and transfer the chicken to a serving platter. Set the skillet over medium heat and simmer the sauce, stirring often, until it bubbles and thickens, about 5 minutes. Serve the chicken with the sauce.

chile-rubbed turkey
with cellophane noodle stuffing

Cellophane noodle stuffing? Yes, that's right, get ready to have your Thanksgiving expectations blown out of the water! The cellophane noodles lighten the texture of the bread stuffing and give it a bouncy (in a good way) quality. The bird is rubbed with ground Thai bird's eye chiles, paprika, and salt and dry brines in the fridge for a few hours, enough time for the salt to tenderize the meat and give it a somewhat fiery taste. The meat ends up being so juicy and flavorful, you won't even need gravy, though a few pickles (see pages 134 to 144) are always nice.

CHILE-BRINED TURKEY

1 (12- to 15-pound) turkey

2½ tablespoons sweet paprika

2 tablespoons kosher salt

2 tablespoons ground dried Thai
    bird's eye chile

½ tablespoon freshly ground
    black pepper

2 medium carrots, cut into thirds

1 medium yellow onion, quartered

8 garlic cloves, smashed

1½ cups chicken broth

½ cup apple cider vinegar

heads-up

It's very important to let the turkey come up to room temperature before roasting so the bird cooks evenly and the breast meat doesn't dry out. It could take anywhere from 3 to 6 hours, depending on the size of your turkey, it to lose its chill, so plan accordingly.

1   **BRINE THE TURKEY:** Rinse the inside and outside of the turkey under cold running water (remove the bag in the cavity with the giblets and neck and save them for making gravy or discard), then pat dry with paper towels. Mix the paprika, salt, ground chile, and pepper together in a small bowl, then pat the spice mixture all over the entire surface of the turkey so the skin is nicely coated. Refrigerate the turkey on a baking sheet or in a roasting pan overnight.

2   Remove the turkey from the refrigerator and tie the base of the drumsticks together with butcher's twine. Tuck the wings behind the breast and set the turkey on a lightly greased roasting rack set into a roasting pan. Let the turkey come up to room temperature, 3 to 6 hours (depending on how warm your kitchen is and how large the bird is).

3   **TOAST THE BREAD CUBES FOR THE CELLOPHANE NOODLE STUFFING:** Preheat the oven to 350°F. Toss the bread cubes with 2 tablespoons of the oil in a large bowl. Turn the cubes out onto a rimmed baking sheet and dry them out in the oven until crisp and golden, about 15 minutes, stirring midway through toasting. Remove from the oven and set aside.

4   **ROAST THE TURKEY:** Increase the oven temperature to 475°F. Cover the wings of the turkey with aluminum foil and add the

recipe continues

CELLOPHANE NOODLE STUFFING

4 cups roughly torn sourdough bread cubes or store-bought bread crumbs

4 tablespoons extra-virgin olive oil

1 pound cellophane noodles

1 large yellow onion, finely diced

6 garlic cloves, very finely chopped

2 tablespoons lightly packed light brown sugar

1½ teaspoons kosher salt

2 teaspoons freshly ground black pepper

3 medium carrots, very finely diced into small cubes

3 celery stalks, very finely diced into small cubes

½ cup finely diced white button mushroom caps (5 to 6 medium)

8 tablespoons (4 ounces) unsalted butter

1 cup chicken broth

3 cups coarsely chopped fresh flat-leaf parsley leaves

carrots, onion, and garlic to the bottom of the roasting pan. Place the turkey in the oven and roast for 30 minutes. Add the broth and vinegar to the roasting pan, reduce the oven temperature to 350°F, and loosely tent breast with foil. Continue to roast the turkey, basting it with the pan juices every 20 to 30 minutes, until the thickest part of the breast registers 140°F on an instant-read thermometer, about 1½ hours (the turkey will get stuffed at this point, then will finish roasting in the oven).

5   **WHILE THE TURKEY ROASTS, MAKE THE STUFFING:** Cook the cellophane noodles according to the package instructions, then transfer them to a colander and rinse them under cold water, shaking off the excess liquid; place the noodles in a large bowl.

6   Heat the remaining 2 tablespoons of oil in a large skillet over medium-high heat until it shimmers, about 2 minutes. Add the onion and garlic and cook, stirring often, until the onion starts to brown around the edges, 3 to 4 minutes. Reduce the heat to medium and stir in the brown sugar, salt, and pepper. Continue to cook, stirring often, until the onion is nicely browned, 2 to 3 minutes more (if the sugar starts to stick or burn, reduce the heat to medium-low). Stir in the carrots and celery and cook for 3 minutes, then stir in the mushrooms and turn off the heat. Transfer the stuffing to the bowl with the noodles and toss to combine.

7   Melt the butter in a medium saucepan over medium heat. Add the chicken broth and bring the mixture to a gentle simmer. Turn off the heat and pour the broth mixture over the noodle-stuffing mixture and stir to combine. Remove the turkey from the oven and pack as much of the cellophane stuffing into the turkey cavity as will fit; put the remaining stuffing in a separate baking dish.

8   Return the turkey and the baking dish with the extra stuffing to the oven and continue to roast until the temperature in the thickest part of the breast registers 155°F on an instant-read thermometer, 20 to 30 minutes more. Remove the turkey from the oven and loosely tent with foil for at least 30 minutes before transferring the stuffing to a serving dish and carving the turkey. Serve the vegetables and pan drippings alongside the turkey, if you like. Stir the parsley into the stuffing before serving.

crispy-skin duck breast with black plum chutney

When cooking duck breasts, we choose large Moulard breasts that clock in around one pound each. Moulards are less fatty than Pekin duck breasts and the meat has a softer, less gamy flavor than Muscovy breasts. For the crispiest skin and perfectly rare to medium-rare meat, there are a few key techniques to keep in mind. First, when scoring the skin and fat (this helps render off the fat), do it in a tight diamond or crosshatch pattern, slicing only halfway through the fat. The un-scored fat layer helps protect the meat during the low-and-slow cooking process. Second, cook the duck breast with care over very low heat. Go too fast and you'll burn the skin while overcooking the meat and not rendering off all the fat. Third, before flipping the breast to the meat side, pour off the duck fat (save it for roasting potatoes) and finish the meaty side in butter. Why? Because it tastes good.

DUCK BREASTS

12 whole star anise

3 tablespoons whole black peppercorns

2 large duck breasts (preferably from Moulard ducks), fat trimmed so it perfectly aligns to the breast meat

2 teaspoons kosher salt

3½ tablespoons unsalted butter

(Not Really) Basic Rice (page 165), for serving

PLUM CHUTNEY

1 tablespoon canola oil

1 small shallot, very finely chopped

1½ teaspoons finely chopped peeled fresh ginger

3 black plums, halved, pitted, and chopped

2 tablespoons golden raisins

¼ teaspoon kosher salt

¼ teaspoon freshly ground black pepper

1 to 2 teaspoons apple cider vinegar

Thai basil or Italian basil, for serving

1   **SPICE THE DUCK BREASTS:** Combine the star anise and peppercorns in a spice grinder and pulverize until fine. Set aside 1 tablespoon of the mixture for the plum chutney.

2   Set the duck breasts on a cutting board. Use a sharp knife to score the skin on an angle halfway down through the fat layer in ½- to ¾-inch intervals. Repeat going in the opposite direction so you have a diamond crosshatch effect. Place the breasts fat-side down in a container. Rub the meat with the remaining anise-pepper mixture (take care not to get spices on the skin or fat), cover the container, and refrigerate for at least 4 hours or up to overnight.

3   **MAKE THE PLUM CHUTNEY:** In a medium saucepan, heat the oil over medium heat. Add the reserved ground spice mixture and once it's fragrant, 15 to 30 seconds, add the shallot and ginger. Cook, stirring often, until the shallot softens, making sure it doesn't brown (if it begins to get dark, reduce the heat to medium-low). Stir in the plums and raisins and cook until the plums begin to break down and the raisins get very soft, about 30 minutes.

recipe continues

heads-up

The duck breasts need to sit with
the spice rub for at least 4 hours or
overnight.

num pang it

Holy Trinity (page 39), toasted baguette

4   Transfer the chutney to a food processor, add the salt and
    pepper, and pulse to combine. Add 1 teaspoon of the vinegar,
    pulse, and taste. The chutney should be sweet with a back note of
    sour—if the vinegar doesn't comes through, add an extra ½ to
    1 teaspoon. Transfer the chutney to a medium bowl and set aside
    or refrigerate until serving.

5   Remove the duck breasts from the refrigerator. Use a paper
    towel to wipe off any spice that may have gotten on the fat
    side. Sprinkle the salt over the meat side of each breast. Set a
    small skillet over medium-high heat for 1 minute, then place the
    duck breasts fat-side down in the pan. As soon as you hear the
    fat sizzle, reduce the heat to medium-low. Slowly render the
    fat, pouring the excess fat into a heat-safe container as it pools,
    every 5 to 6 minutes or so (you don't want the meat to deep-fry
    in the fat). Depending on how much fat the duck breast has, it
    could take anywhere from 15 to 30 minutes to render off 75 to 80
    percent of the fat. Pour off any fat in the skillet and add the butter
    to the pan. Once the butter is melted and foamy, turn the breasts
    meat-side down and cook the duck breasts, using tongs to turn
    the breasts in the butter, for 15 to 30 seconds, just enough to
    lightly cook the surface of the meat (if you place the breast, meat-
    side up, on a plate, the meat should give to slight pressure but not
    feel fleshy). Transfer the breasts to a cutting board and tent with
    aluminum foil for 5 minutes.

6   Slice the duck breasts crosswise into thin pieces. Serve with
    steamed rice, the plum chutney, and basil.

michael anthony's epic duck meat loaf

Let's start by stating the obvious: this is not your mom's, grandma's, great-aunt's, or even your food-obsessed best friend's meat loaf—this meat loaf comes from one of New York City's most talented chefs, Michael Anthony of Gramercy Tavern and Untitled, who developed it for us as part of our charity-driven Guest Chef program (see page 59 for more information). Ben and Mike met at a gym and quickly connected over restaurant stories—getting Mike involved with the Guest Chef program was a no-brainer. The meat loaf component is actually more like a duck pâté, made with duck meat, pork fat, and chicken offal (like liver and hearts). It's really full and complex, and yes, it takes time to make, but it's incredibly special and totally worth it. The homemade kimchi is excellent, too. So why not just devote a rainy afternoon to making it? The kimchi will pay off in dividends stashed away in the fridge, whether you pair it with the meat loaf, or eat it with an omelet, fried rice (page 166), or straight from the container. Michael dedicated his share of the charitable contribution from the sale of the Gramercy Pang to God's Love We Deliver, an organization devoted to improving the health and nutrition of people living with AIDS and other serious illnesses. Num Pang made a contribution to the Food Bank for New York City.

KIMCHI

1¼ heads napa cabbage, outer leaves removed, heads halved lengthwise

1 cup fine sea salt

1 (4-inch) piece kombu

1 cup bonito flakes

½ cup sweet rice flour

1 jalapeño, coarsely chopped

1 medium yellow onion, coarsely chopped

½ cup coarsely chopped garlic

¼ cup coarsely chopped peeled fresh ginger

1 cup Korean red chile powder (*gochugaru*)

¼ cup fish sauce

¼ cup salted dried shrimp (see The Num Pang Pantry, page 25)

¼ cup store-bought bottled clam juice

1 pound daikon, peeled and cut into thin matchsticks

½ bunch fresh chives, cut into 2-inch lengths

4 scallions, cut into 2-inch lengths

1   **SALT THE CABBAGE FOR THE KIMCHI:** Place the cabbage in a very large container. Add ½ cup of the sea salt and lukewarm water to cover and let the mixture sit out at room temperature overnight. Remove the cabbage from the salted water and sprinkle the remaining ½ cup sea salt between the leaves. Return the cabbage to the salted water and let it sit overnight at room temperature.

2   Drain and rinse the cabbage under cold water. Be gentle but thorough (it will be very salty if not rinsed well). Squeeze as much water from the cabbage as possible. Place the cabbage on a wire rack set on top of a rimmed baking sheet. Cover with plastic wrap and let the cabbage drain for 1 hour.

3   **WHILE THE CABBAGE IS DRAINING, MAKE DASHI FOR THE KIMCHI:** In a large pot, warm 4 cups water over medium-low heat until it is warm to the touch but not hot. Reduce the heat to low, add the kombu, set a lid on the pot so it sits slightly askew, and warm the liquid gently for 45 minutes (do not simmer or boil). Turn off the heat and add the bonito flakes, steep for 5 minutes, then drain into a fine-mesh sieve set over a bowl (you should end up with at least 3 cups of dashi).

recipe continues

MEAT LOAF

2 tablespoons grapeseed oil

½ medium yellow onion, finely chopped

6 garlic cloves, very finely chopped

1½ tablespoons dried oregano

1½ teaspoons fennel seeds

1½ teaspoons whole black peppercorns

½ teaspoon celery seeds

1 pound lean duck meat (such as tenders or skinless duck breast)

7 ounces chilled pork fat, cut into 1-inch cubes

3½ ounces chicken gizzards

3½ ounces chicken hearts

3½ ounces chicken livers

2 large eggs, lightly beaten

¼ cup Japanese panko bread crumbs

2 teaspoons red wine vinegar

2 tablespoons finely chopped fresh flat-leaf parsley

1 tablespoon kosher salt

4   **MAKE THE KIMCHI:** Whisk 1 cup of the dashi and the sweet rice flour together in a large pot until smooth. Warm the mixture over medium-high heat, stirring often. When the mixture is warm to the touch (don't boil it), reduce the heat to low and slowly add the remaining 2 cups dashi. The mixture should immediately thicken and become translucent. Turn off the heat and set the mixture aside.

5   In a food processor, combine the jalapeño, onion, garlic, and ginger and pulse until finely chopped. Transfer this mixture to a large container and whisk in the dashi mixture, the chile powder, fish sauce, dried shrimp, and clam juice. Add the daikon, chives, and scallions.

6   Line a large plastic container with a plastic bag. Place a head of cabbage in the container and apply the marinade between the leaves, working from the tips of the leaves to the core and filling the space between each leaf without overstuffing. Fold the tops of the outer leaves down toward the core, making little kimchi bundles. Repeat with the remaining heads of cabbage. Press down on the cabbage, then tie the plastic bag shut. Leave some headspace in the bag, as the kimchi will expand as it ferments. Place a weight on top of the bag (a large heavy plate works well) to keep the kimchi submerged and refrigerate for at least 4 days. Transfer the kimchi to two airtight quart-size containers and refrigerate for up to 3 weeks.

7   **MAKE THE MEAT LOAF:** Place the parts for a meat grinder including a 5-mm die in the freezer to chill. Heat the oil in a medium skillet over medium-high heat. Add the onion, reduce the heat to medium, and cook, stirring often, until the onion is translucent, 2 to 3 minutes. Stir in the garlic and continue to cook until the onion is golden and soft and the garlic is fragrant, about 2 minutes more (reduce

the heat if the onion or garlic starts to brown). Transfer to a medium bowl to cool. Once cool, add the oregano, fennel seeds, peppercorns, and celery seeds. Stir in the duck meat, pork fat, gizzards, hearts, and livers. Cover the bowl with plastic wrap and refrigerate until the mixture is completely cold, at least 3 hours or overnight.

8   Set up the meat grinder and grind the chilled meat and aromatics. Collect everything in a medium bowl and use your hands to work in the eggs, panko, vinegar, parsley, and salt, kneading the mixture until it is well combined. Be sure to keep this mixture very cold (below 38°F is ideal), returning the mixture to the refrigerator if it becomes too warm.

9   Preheat the oven to 325°F. Line a 1½-quart terrine mold with plastic wrap. Fill the terrine with the meat loaf mixture, patting it down and lightly knocking the bottom of the mold against your counter to eliminate air pockets. Set the terrine mold in a large roasting pan and add enough hot water to reach halfway up the sides of the mold. Set the roasting pan in the oven and cook until the internal temperature of the meat loaf registers 138°F on an instant-read thermometer, about 1 hour and 15 minutes.

10   Remove the roasting pan from the oven and carefully lift out the terrine mold. Set the meat loaf aside for 45 minutes to cool, then refrigerate until cold.

11   Preheat the oven to 350°F. Line a rimmed baking sheet with aluminum foil. Invert the meat loaf onto a cutting board and remove the plastic wrap. Slice it crosswise into 1½-inch pieces and set the pieces on the prepared baking sheet. Place the meat loaf in the oven until it is warmed through. Serve alongside a generous amount of kimchi.

PIG

pulled pork with spicy honey

From the very first day we opened, this sandwich has been one of our most popular *num pang*s. It's like our take on Southern barbecue, with fish sauce and sambal lending heat and that distinct sweet-sour Southeast Asian flavor. You could absolutely try this out in a slow cooker—we imagine that this is just the kind of recipe that slow cookers were invented for.

PULLED PORK

1 (5-pound) bone-in pork butt

¼ cup chile powder (from dried and ground red chiles)

¼ cup kosher salt

2 tablespoons freshly ground black pepper

1½ medium yellow onions, sliced crosswise into 1-inch rings

15 garlic cloves, smashed

2 cups orange juice (preferably freshly squeezed)

2 cups apple cider vinegar

SPICY HONEY SAUCE

1¼ cups honey

1 cup orange juice (preferably freshly squeezed)

¼ cup apple cider vinegar

2 tablespoons sambal oelek (see The Num Pang Pantry, page 29)

2 tablespoons fish sauce

Assorted pickles, for serving (pages 134 to 144)

Steamed jasmine rice, for serving

1   **MAKE THE PULLED PORK:** Preheat the oven to 250°F. Set the pork butt on a cutting board. In a small bowl, mix together the chili powder, salt, and pepper and then rub the blend all over the pork. Place the onions and garlic cloves in the bottom of a large Dutch oven or roasting pan and set the pork on top. Add the orange juice, vinegar, and 1 cup water, cover with a lid or aluminum foil, and braise until the pork pulls apart easily with a fork, 5 to 6 hours.

2   Remove the pork from the oven and let cool. When it is cool enough to handle, transfer it to a cutting board and use two forks to pull the meat off the bone and shred it. Set aside (the pork can be refrigerated for up to 3 days before serving). Strain the braising liquid through a fine-mesh sieve and set aside, then skim off the fat that rises to the surface.

3   **MAKE THE SPICY HONEY SAUCE:** In a medium bowl, whisk together the honey, orange juice, vinegar, sambal, fish sauce, and the reserved defatted braising liquid.

4   Preheat the oven to 350°F. In a large bowl, combine the shredded pork with the spicy honey sauce. Place the pork in a baking dish and bake until it is completely heated through, about 40 minutes. Drain off any fat in the baking dish, then serve with assorted pickles and rice.

recipe continues

VARIATION: NUM CUBANO Spread some chili mayo (page 40) inside each toasted baguette, evenly coating both the top and bottom sides. Add some pulled pork and 2 slices of deli ham to the bottom half of each baguette. Top with 1½ slices of Swiss cheese, then some pickled carrots (page 42). To the top baguette half, add a smear of yellow mustard, a few cucumber slices, a few Spicy Pickled Kirbies (page 144), and cilantro sprigs. Sandwich the two halves together and serve.

heads-up

Bank on 5 to 6 hours in the oven for the pork butt to become tender.

num pang it

Holy Trinity (page 39), toasted baguette

crispy pork shoulder

We care about pork shoulder. We care about its tenderness, which is why we marinate a pork butt (also called a Boston butt) overnight in a vinegar and spicy chile broth, letting the acid in the liquid tenderize the meat so after it's done roasting, it will be so tender it practically falls apart on your tongue. We care about the crispness of its skin, which is why we baby it, to get the crackling-est cracklings. We care about how you eat it—sliced and served on a *num pang*; added to a noodle bowl; with rice alongside; tucked into a summer baguette (page 43). We care.

1 (3- to 3½-pound) bone-in pork butt

1½ tablespoons five-spice powder (see The Num Pang Pantry, page 28)

¼ cup plus 2 teaspoons kosher salt

2 tablespoons packed light brown sugar

¼ teaspoon cayenne pepper

¼ teaspoon freshly ground black pepper

3 tablespoons hoisin sauce

2 tablespoons distilled white vinegar

Tuk Trey Sauce (page 168), for dipping

heads-up

The shoulder needs at least 6 hours to cure, so be sure to account for that when you're planning to make the recipe.

num pang it

Holy Trinity (page 39), toasted baguette

1   Place the pork butt on a cutting board, skin-side up. Score the skin crosswise in 1-inch intervals about 1 inch deep. Mix the five-spice powder, 2 teaspoons of the salt, the brown sugar, cayenne, and black pepper together in a small bowl and pat it onto the meat side and between the slits. Then rub with the hoisin sauce. Place the butt in an airtight container, skin-side up. Mix the remaining ¼ cup salt with the vinegar and pat some of the mixture onto the skin. Cover the container and refrigerate the pork overnight. (Cover the remaining salt-vinegar solution with plastic wrap and set aside at room temperature overnight.)

2   Remove the pork from the refrigerator and preheat the oven to 325°F. Line a baking dish with aluminum foil.

3   Place the pork skin-side up in the prepared baking dish and brush off the salt. Reapply some of the reserved salt-vinegar mixture and place the pork in the oven. Bake for 30 minutes, then remove the pork from the oven and increase the oven temperature to 400°F. Continue to roast until the skin is covered with sizzling, blistering bubbles and a knife easily slides into the meat (the skin will be quite hard and crisp, so insert the knife at an angle through one of the incisions), 1½ to 2 hours longer. If the skin starts to get too dark, reduce the oven temperature to 350°F.

4   Remove the pork from the oven, set it on a cutting board, and let it rest for 10 minutes. Turn the roast meat-side up and slice around the bone into ½-inch-thick pieces. Serve with the Tuk Trey Sauce on the side.

glazed five-spice pork belly

The sweet-glazed five-spice pork belly is the most popular sandwich at Num Pang. The belly (uncured bacon) is rubbed with a five-spice and sugar mixture and maple syrup, then it gets braised with apples, ginger, and cider for a long, long time. We use leftover braising liquid from making our pulled pork to make the syrupy five-spice glaze, but since you probably won't have that collagen-rich glaze hanging out in your fridge, we show you how to get the same result with beef or chicken stock and a few veal bones. In the fall and winter, we serve the belly with Pickled Asian Pears (page 140) because the acidity of the pickle helps cut through the richness of the pork and the intensity of the glaze; in the spring and summer we add rhubarb to the pickle for a more seasonal take. Save any bits and pieces to make Shrimp Summer Rolls (page 148) or to add to Green Papaya Salad (page 200).

PORK BELLY

½ cup kosher salt

½ cup sugar

1 tablespoon five-spice powder (see The Num Pang Pantry, page 28)

1 (3- to 3½-pound) pork belly, skin removed

½ cup maple syrup

1 apple, halved crosswise, then one half sliced into 2 rounds (save the other half for another use—or eat it!), seeds, skin, and all

1 medium yellow onion, halved crosswise, then one half sliced into 2 rounds (save the other half for another use)

3 dried red chiles

1 (2-inch) piece fresh ginger, cut lengthwise into ¼-inch-thick pieces

3 to 4 cups apple cider

GLAZE

8 cups chicken stock or leftover braising liquid from Pulled Pork with Spicy Honey (page 73)

1½ pounds veal bones (only if using stock; if using the braising liquid, you don't need veal bones)

ingredients continue

1 **MAKE THE PORK BELLY:** Combine the salt, sugar, and five-spice powder in a medium bowl. Set the pork belly on a work surface and rub it down with the cure. Don't be shy—rub the belly for a good 30 seconds on each side. Place the spiced belly in a large airtight container, bowl, or pot and pour the maple syrup over the belly, turning the pork over a couple of times to make sure both sides are nicely coated with the syrup. Cover the container and refrigerate for 12 to 24 hours.

2 Adjust an oven rack to the lower-middle position and preheat the oven to 250°F.

3 Remove the pork belly from the cure, rinse it under cold running water, and pat dry with paper towels. Put the apple, onion, chiles, and ginger in the bottom of a large, heavy-bottomed pot or braising pan. Add the pork belly, fatty-side up, and add enough apple cider to fill the pot 1 inch. Cover with aluminum foil, crimping the edges to seal the pot, and braise the belly until a fork easily slides into the thickest part with no resistance, about 12 hours.

4 **MAKE THE GLAZE:** Meanwhile, pour the stock into a large saucepan. Add the veal bones (if using the braising liquid, you don't need the veal bones), bring to a boil over high heat, reduce

recipe continues

⅓ cup apple cider vinegar

¼ cup finely chopped peeled fresh ginger

1½ teaspoons five-spice powder (see The Num Pang Pantry, page 28)

1 small dried red chile

⅓ cup maple syrup

KNOW THIS: IF YOU DON'T MAKE IT, FAKE IT

The consistency of the glaze depends on the amount of natural collagen (gelatin) in the stock that you're using to make it. Stock, which is made with lots of bones, typically has a greater amount of collagen in it and, when reduced, will yield a thicker sauce. We use the rich-and-lustrous leftover liquid from braising the pulled pork on page 73 to make the glaze for the Glazed Five-Spice Pork Belly, but we realize not everyone has stock in the house, so yes, you *can* substitute broth, but know you might have to thicken the glaze with cornstarch. If your glaze does end up on the thin side, stir in a slurry of 2 teaspoons cornstarch dissolved in 2 tablespoons water. Let it simmer for 1 to 2 minutes, or until the glaze has a nice sheen. If it thickens too much, loosen it with a little more chicken stock, broth, or water.

to medium-low, and cook, skimming the surface every 20 minutes to remove any impurities that rise to the top, until the stock has reduced by about a third, 2 to 2½ hours.

5   Remove the belly from the braising liquid and strain the braising liquid into an 8-cup liquid measuring cup. Let the belly and braising liquid cool to room temperature. Slice the belly crosswise into rib-size portions.

6   Use a spoon to skim the fat off from the top of the braising liquid. Add enough of the veal bone stock to the defatted braising liquid to yield 6 cups of liquid total, then pour it into a medium saucepan (save any extra stock to use another time). Stir in half the vinegar, the ginger, five-spice powder, and chile and bring to a simmer over medium-high heat. Reduce the heat to medium-low and cook until the glaze has reduced by two-thirds, 30 to 45 minutes. Turn off the heat and add the maple syrup. Taste and adjust with more vinegar, if needed.

7   Adjust the oven rack to the upper-middle position, set a rimmed baking sheet on the rack, and heat the broiler to high. Set the pieces of pork belly on the hot baking sheet. After a few minutes, and once the fat starts to sizzle, remove the baking sheet from the oven and brush a generous amount of glaze over each piece of pork. Return the baking sheet to the oven and once the glaze sizzles, 1 to 2 minutes (watch the pork closely, as broiler intensities vary), remove the pork from the oven and serve.

heads-up

This recipe requires overnight curing and 12 hours braising, plus 45 minutes to make the glaze (using the braising liquid). It's worth it, trust us. (And be sure to save a bit for breakfast sandwiches, page 85, the next morning!)

num pang it

Holy Trinity (page 39), Pickled Asian Pears (page 140), toasted baguette

khmer sausage patties

Ben started the Brooklyn Bangers sausage company in 2012 with his Brooklyn-based restaurant group partners. Along with cheddar bratwursts, smoked hot dogs, and kielbasa, they also started making Khmer-style sausages for Num Pang. Cilantro, ground Thai bird's eye chiles, fish sauce, and fresh ginger are a few seasonings that make the sausages unique—on a bun with the traditional *num pang* add-ons like pickled carrots, cucumber slices, and chili mayo, it's a spectacular sandwich. Most home cooks don't have the time (or desire) to make sausages—so here's our patty hack version that's just as easy as making meatballs. Freeze a few patties to make the breakfast sandwich on page 85.

1½ pounds ground pork

¼ cup finely chopped fresh cilantro

3 garlic cloves, finely chopped or pressed through a garlic press

2 tablespoons plus 1½ teaspoons coconut or palm sugar

1 tablespoon finely chopped peeled fresh ginger

1 tablespoon plus 1½ teaspoons panko bread crumbs

1 teaspoon pulverized dried shiitake mushrooms or porcini mushrooms

3 tablespoons soy sauce

2 tablespoons fish sauce

2 teaspoons Sriracha sauce

¼ teaspoon ground dried Thai bird's eye chile

¼ cup canola oil, plus more as needed

heads-up

After mixing the meat with the herbs and seasonings, it needs a half hour in the fridge to let the flavors come together before cooking.

num pang it

Holy Trinity (page 39), toasted baguette

1   Place the pork in a large bowl and add the cilantro, garlic, sugar, ginger, bread crumbs, mushrooms, soy sauce, fish sauce, Sriracha, and ground chile. Use your hands to knead the mixture together until well combined. Cover the mixture with plastic wrap pressed directly against the surface and refrigerate for 30 minutes.

2   Remove the bowl from the fridge and make a small slider-sized patty from the meat mixture (this will be used to test for seasoning, so don't make it too big). In a large skillet, heat 1 tablespoon of the oil over medium-high heat. Add the test patty and cook on both sides until browned and the sausage is cooked through, 5 to 6 minutes total. Turn off the heat and transfer the patty to a paper towel–lined plate to drain, then try it. If the mixture needs more chile, hot sauce, or soy sauce, add it to the bowl with the remaining raw sausage mixture and knead it in. Now divide the mixture into 10 equal-size portions and form them into rounds, then flatten them into ½-inch-thick patties.

3   Add 2 tablespoons of the remaining oil to the skillet and set the pan over medium-high heat. Add enough patties to fill the pan without crowding it, then reduce the heat to medium and cook the patties on both sides until browned and cooked through, 6 to 8 minutes total. Transfer to the paper towel–lined plate to drain. Add more oil to the pan as needed and cook the remaining sausage patties. Serve hot.

guinness-maple–glazed peach and bacon num pang

Everyone knows salty and sweet work so well together—but add the stickiness of the glaze and the crunch of the bacon against the suppleness of the grilled peach and it's just like . . . wow. This *num pang* is on our menu for the blink of an eye, appearing once peach season is in full swing in the Northeast, and disappearing once the peaches do. Make it while you can and savor every bite, because before you know it, peach season is done.

GUINNESS-MAPLE GLAZE

3 (14.9-ounce) cans Guinness beer

1½ cups honey

½ cup maple syrup

3 garlic cloves, smashed

2 small yellow onions, quartered

1 ripe peach, halved, pitted, and thinly sliced

Heaping ¼ cup coarsely chopped peeled fresh ginger

1 tablespoon freshly ground black pepper

2 small dried red chiles, smashed

NUM PANG

8 thick-cut bacon slices

2 tablespoons extra-virgin olive oil

6 scallions, halved lengthwise

1 jalapeño, thinly sliced

½ teaspoon kosher salt, plus more for peaches

Pinch of freshly ground black pepper plus more for peaches

Pinch of sugar

3 ripe medium peaches, halved, pitted, and halved again (so you have 12 pieces)

4 (6-inch) baguettes, split lengthwise and toasted

½ cup Most Important Chili Mayo (page 40)

1 **MAKE THE GUINNESS-MAPLE GLAZE:** In a large saucepan, combine the Guinness, honey, maple syrup, garlic, onions, peach, ginger, pepper, and chiles. Bring to a boil over high heat, then reduce the heat to medium-low and simmer until the sauce is thick and has the consistency of a glaze, 30 to 40 minutes. Transfer the mixture to a blender and puree, then set aside to cool.

2 **MAKE THE NUM PANG:** Preheat the oven to 400°F. Line a rimmed baking sheet with aluminum foil. Place the bacon on the baking sheet and bake until golden-brown, 15 to 20 minutes. Transfer the bacon to a paper towel–lined plate to drain and set aside.

3 In a medium skillet, heat 1 tablespoon of the oil over medium heat. Add the scallions, jalapeño, salt, pepper, and sugar and cook, stirring occasionally, until the scallions start to brown, 3 to 4 minutes. Turn off the heat and set aside.

4 Reduce the oven temperature to 350°F. Place the peaches in a large bowl and toss with the remaining 1 tablespoon oil. Season with salt and pepper. Heat a charcoal or gas grill to medium-high or set a grill pan over medium-high heat. Grill the peaches until they are marked on both sides, about 2 minutes total. Transfer the peaches to a baking dish so they rest in a single layer, then pour 1 cup of the glaze over the peaches. Return the peaches to the oven until the glaze becomes bubbly and starts to caramelize, 15 to 20 minutes.

2 medium Kirby cucumbers, thinly
   sliced lengthwise on an angle to
   make 6 long planks

Fresh cilantro sprigs

1 cup Holy Pickled Carrots (page 42)

heads-up

Take care not to overgrill the peaches.
Small peaches might need a little less
time; large peaches can probably go a
little longer. Nectarines work too.

5   Spread both sides of each baguette with chili mayo. To the top
half, add a few cucumber slices followed by a few cilantro sprigs
and ¼ cup of the pickled carrots. Set 3 peaches on the bottom
half of each baguette. Top with the sautéed scallions and bacon.
Cover with the top half of the baguette and serve.

breakfast egg and sausage pang

We have always been huge fans of the classic New York City sandwich: the bacon, egg, and cheese. Our favorite version calls for the Khmer Sausage Patties on page 81, flavored with ginger, garlic, sesame oil, and all kinds of good Cambodian accents. If you aren't up to making the Khmer sausage (we all have *those* kind of mornings), just use your favorite store-bought breakfast sausage instead. There are so many flavorful toppings in the egg component and on the sandwich—like Chili Yogurt (page 40), fried onions, and fresh cilantro—that it will still be really, really good.

1 tablespoon canola oil

8 large eggs

2 scallions, thinly sliced

¼ cup finely chopped fresh cilantro leaves

1 tablespoon black sesame seeds

1 tablespoon soy sauce

1 tablespoon Sriracha sauce

½ teaspoon freshly ground black pepper

¼ teaspoon kosher salt

4 brioche buns, split

4 cooked breakfast sausage patties, sliced Glazed Five-Spice Pork Belly (page 78), or Khmer Sausage Patties (page 81)

Chili Yogurt (page 40), for serving

Store-bought fried onions, for serving

Fresh cilantro sprigs, for serving

heads-up

We use very crispy fried shallots to top the sandwich, but store-bought fried onions (like the kind you put on top of the green bean casserole at Thanksgiving!) are good, too. Believe us—no one will complain.

1   Preheat the oven to 350°F. Lightly coat an 8-inch square baking dish or nonstick 8-inch square cake pan with the oil and set aside.

2   In a large bowl, whisk together the eggs, scallions, chopped cilantro, sesame seeds, soy sauce, Sriracha, pepper, and salt. Pour the egg mixture into the baking dish and bake for 7 minutes. Rotate the pan and continue to bake the eggs until the edges are set and puffy and the center jiggles slightly when the pan is tapped, about 10 minutes more. Remove the pan from the oven and cool for 10 minutes.

3   Meanwhile, broil, grill, or toast the brioche buns on their cut sides until lightly golden or grill marked. Set aside.

4   Invert the slightly cooled baked egg square onto a cutting board, then cut it into quarters. Slide a sausage patty onto the bottom of a brioche bun. Add a square of egg on top. To the top bun half, add the chili yogurt, then sprinkle with some fried onions and top with a few cilantro sprigs. Carefully turn the top half over the bottom half and serve.

mario batali's cotechino sausage and pickled balsamic onion num pang

Before we opened Num Pang, Mario Batali of Babbo, Del Posto, and Eataly (among so many other restaurants around the world) frequented Kampuchea, and when we opened Num Pang on 12th Street, he became a regular (we heard he likes to bring the cauliflower *pang* with him on flights), so it made sense to reach out to him to be our very first chef collaborator for our Guest Chef program (see page 59). Mario made these killer homemade sausages for his *pang*— it's a bit of a process to make sausage, but once you go down that road, don't be surprised if you get hooked. The money raised from this *num pang* went to benefit the Cambodian Children's Fund and the Food Bank for New York City.

SAUSAGE

7 pounds pork shoulder

3 pounds pork skin

2 pounds pork back fat

1 cup grated Parmigiano-Reggiano cheese

8 garlic cloves, very finely chopped

6 tablespoons table salt

3 tablespoons freshly ground black pepper

1 tablespoon cayenne pepper

1 tablespoon ground cinnamon

1 tablespoon freshly grated nutmeg

1 teaspoon ground cloves

2 cups ice water

10 feet 55-mm beef middle casings

2 cinnamon sticks

2 tablespoons whole coriander seeds

1   **MAKE THE SAUSAGE:** Place the parts for a meat grinder (use a 55-mm die) in the freezer to chill. Place the pork shoulder, pork skin, and back fat in a bowl and chill in the freezer for 30 minutes, then cut into pieces small enough to fit through a meat grinder.

2   In a large bowl, mix together the Parmigiano-Reggiano, garlic, salt, black pepper, cayenne, ground cinnamon, nutmeg, cloves, and ice water. Set up the meat grinder with the chilled equipment from the freezer and grind the chilled chopped pork, adding it to the bowl with the spices and ice water. Knead the meat and spices together until well combined. Cover with plastic wrap and refrigerate overnight.

3   Place the casings in a large bowl of cool water and set aside for 5 minutes, drain, and one by one, open each casing and use the kitchen sink faucet to flush them out. Load one 20-inch length of casing onto a sausage stuffer and tie off the bottom with a piece of butcher's twine. Fill the casing with the chilled meat mixture until the casing is pretty full and about 2 inches are left on the other end. Move your hand down along the sausage and toward the tied end to compact the filling and ensure there aren't any air pockets, then twist the long sausage into two 9-inch links. Tie off the other end with butcher's twine and repeat with the remaining casings and meat mixture. Place the sausages in a deep roasting pan filled with cold water and refrigerate overnight.

MARINATED ONIONS

3 medium red onions, cut into ⅛-inch-
thick rings

1½ cups balsamic vinegar

1 cup ice water

¾ cup sugar

2 tablespoons red pepper flakes

2 tablespoons finely chopped fresh
rosemary

NUM PANG

4 (6-inch) baguettes, split lengthwise
and toasted

3 tablespoons Most Important
Chili Mayo (page 40)

8 to 12 superthin slices Cacio di Roma
cheese

1 medium Kirby cucumber, thinly
sliced lengthwise on an angle into
6 long planks

⅔ cup Holy Pickled Carrots (page 42)

8 fresh cilantro sprigs

heads-up

It takes about 3 days and a lot of pork
to make your own cotechino sausage.
Get the beef middle casings from a
butcher or just order them online.
Cacio di Roma cheese is a sheep's-milk
cheese from the Lazio region of Italy—it
melts beautifully.

4   The next day, drain the sausages and prick each one all over with
a pin to prevent the casing from bursting during cooking. Place
the sausages in a shallow 2-quart casserole dish. Cover with cold
water, add the cinnamon sticks and coriander, and bring the water
to a boil over high heat. Reduce the heat to medium-low and
gently simmer until the sausages are milky white and opaque,
about 4 hours. Remove the sausages from the pan and set aside
to cool.

5   **MAKE THE MARINATED ONIONS:** Place the onions, vinegar, ice
water, sugar, red pepper flakes, and rosemary in a large bowl and
toss to combine. Cover with plastic wrap and refrigerate for 1 hour.

6   **MAKE THE NUM PANG:** Spread both sides of each baguette half
with the chili mayo. On the bottom baguette half, add some
marinated onions. Top with a sausage, followed by enough cheese
slices to just cover the sausage. On the other baguette half, add
the cucumber slices followed by the cilantro and the pickled
carrots. Press the two halves together and serve.

orange-glazed spicy pork steak

Pork butt is the cut often reserved for pulled pork; it's cheap, fatty, and tasty, and the usual route of cooking is to braise it for hours and hours until it's fall-apart tender (like for our pulled pork on page 73). Here we go the steak route instead, and thinly slice the butt into steaks (ask your butcher to do it for you), then rub it down with a dry cure made of chiles and salt. After a few hours, the pork goes into a skillet to caramelize with the spicy-smoky glaze. On bread or not, this is good eating.

PORK STEAKS

4 (½-inch-thick) pork butt steaks (about 1½ pounds total)

2 tablespoons kosher salt

2 teaspoons sweet paprika

1 teaspoon cayenne pepper

GLAZE

1 cup orange juice (preferably freshly squeezed)

¼ cup honey

¼ cup soy sauce

¼ cup sambal oelek (see The Num Pang Pantry, page 29)

2 garlic cloves, smashed

1 (2-inch) piece fresh ginger, halved lengthwise and smashed

¼ red or yellow onion (leave intact)

1 teaspoon kosher salt

1 teaspoon ground black pepper

2 teaspoons canola oil

1   **CURE THE PORK STEAKS:** Set the pork steaks on a cutting board and use a paper towel to blot both sides dry. In a small bowl, mix together the salt, paprika, and cayenne. Rub both sides of each pork steak with the spice blend, set in an airtight container, cover, and refrigerate for at least 1 hour or overnight.

2   **MAKE THE GLAZE:** In a medium saucepan, combine the orange juice, honey, soy sauce, sambal, garlic, ginger, onion, salt, and pepper. Bring to a simmer over medium-high heat, reduce the heat to medium-low, and cook until the sauce is the consistency of maple syrup, about 50 minutes.

3   **COOK THE PORK STEAKS:** Heat a large skillet over medium-high heat. Add the oil, and once it shimmers, add the pork steaks. Cook, without moving, until both sides are browned, about 6 minutes total. Add 1 cup of the glaze to the pan and simmer for 1 minute. Turn off the heat. Use tongs to lift the steaks out of the pan and let the excess glaze drip off, then transfer to a cutting board.

4   Slice the pork steaks crosswise against the grain and on an angle. Return the slices to the skillet with the glaze and set over medium-high heat to cook on both sides until caramelized, turning the slices over occasionally to coat both sides with the glaze. Divide among individual plates, using a spoon to drizzle any remaining glaze from the pan over the meat. Serve.

heads-up

Start curing the pork steaks before putting the sauce on to simmer. By the time the sauce has reduced, you can cook the pork steaks. The glaze keeps nicely in the fridge, so feel free to make it up to a week ahead of using.

num pang it

Holy Trinity (page 39), toasted baguette

KNOW THIS: FLAME-ROAST YOUR GINGER

To get a unique and smoked flavor from fresh ginger, oil it up and then use tongs to roast it over a live flame. Turn the ginger often until all sides become slightly charred, then use as the recipe instructs. You can also grill the ginger or set it on a baking sheet and blacken it under the broiler.

BEEF, OX & LAMB

GINGER-BARBECUED BRISKET 91

HOISIN MEATBALLS 95

AD-ROCK PANG 96

GRILLED SKIRT STEAK WITH CRUSHED CORIANDER
    AND PEPPERCORNS 99

BURGER PANG 100

NEW YORK STRIP WITH SCALLION-CHILE SAUCE 101

BRAISED SHORT RIBS AND VINEGARY SCALLIONS
    WITH CAULIFLOWER PUREE 102

LEMONGRASS LEG OF LAMB 104

ginger-barbecued brisket

———

When it comes to cooking brisket, patience is more than a virtue—it's a necessity. Brisket takes several hours in a moderately heated oven to tenderize, but on the upside, using our "meat stack" method (we stack the meat to braise twice as much in half the space), you end up with a lot of brisket to use throughout the week (or freeze for later). Between the two pieces of beef we add mustard seeds and peppercorns, then on top we add a handful of whole garlic cloves and a good amount of sliced ginger. A can of Guinness and some apple cider vinegar make up the braising liquid. After four hours in the oven, this combo of spices, meat, and liquid melds into an incredibly flavorful base that we use to create the ginger barbecue sauce. The brisket is great on a bun or baguette, or shredded and stirred into pasta, used to make hash, or to fill soft tacos.

BRISKET

1 (4-pound) brisket, halved crosswise, or 2 (2-pound) pieces brisket

1½ tablespoons kosher salt

2 medium carrots, peeled and cut into thirds crosswise

1 medium yellow onion, cut crosswise into rings

2 tablespoons brown mustard seeds

2 tablespoons whole black peppercorns

1 (3-inch) piece fresh ginger, thinly sliced lengthwise (no need to peel)

8 garlic cloves

4 cups apple cider vinegar

1 (12-ounce) can Guinness beer

GINGER BARBECUE SAUCE

1 small yellow onion, cut crosswise into ½-inch-thick rings

1 teaspoon canola oil

½ teaspoon kosher salt

Chicken stock, as needed

1 (14-ounce) can whole tomatoes with their juices

2 cups honey

1 cup sugar

1   **BRAISE THE BRISKET:** Preheat the oven to 325°F.

2   Rub both sides of each piece of brisket with the salt. Place the carrots and onion rings in the bottom of a large Dutch oven or roasting pan and add one piece of the brisket. Sprinkle the mustard seeds and peppercorns over the brisket and set the other piece of meat on top. Place the garlic cloves and ginger slices over the top of the brisket, then add the vinegar and beer (it should just cover the meat). Cover the pot (use aluminum foil if using a roasting pan) and braise for 2 hours.

3   Remove the pot from the oven, uncover, and use tongs to reverse the pieces of brisket, moving the bottom piece of brisket to the top of the stack. Re-cover the pot and braise for 2 hours more.

4   Remove the pot from the oven, uncover, and use tongs to reverse the pieces of brisket again. Cover and continue to braise until a fork easily slides into the center of each brisket half, 1½ to 2 hours longer (the brisket braises for a total of 5½ to 6 hours). Transfer the brisket to a cutting board and remove any fat while the meat is still warm. Strain the braising liquid—discard the solids—and set aside to make the sauce .Once the meat is cool, slice the brisket crosswise into 2½-inch-wide pieces. Set aside or refrigerate.

ingredients continue

recipe continues

½ cup apple cider vinegar

⅓ cup coarsely chopped peeled fresh ginger

1 tablespoon soy sauce

1 dried red chile, or ½ teaspoon red pepper flakes

KNOW THIS: REHEAT YOUR MEAT

We work with a lot of slow-cooked meats in the shops—from pork butts and shoulders to pork belly, brisket, and short ribs. After cooking, most any type of meat can be refrigerated for up to 5 days. We like to reheat cold meat gently in the oven. Put the meat on a baking sheet, cover with sauce or some stock or broth, then loosely tent the meat with aluminum foil before setting it in the oven. Let it go until the meat and liquid are both warm, then remove the foil for the last couple of minutes so the whole combination can sizzle and caramelize a bit before serving. For smaller amounts of meat, you can do the same thing in a skillet—put some sauce or broth in a pan, get it warm, add the meat, cover, and warm it ever-so-gently over very low heat (the lowest flame your stovetop can maintain). We recommend running the meat under a broiler for a few minutes before serving.

5 **MAKE THE GINGER BARBECUE SAUCE:** Adjust an oven rack to the top position and preheat the broiler to high. Line a rimmed baking sheet with aluminum foil. Place the onion slices on the baking sheet and toss with the oil. Season with the salt and broil until charred, 2 to 3 minutes (watch the onions closely, as broiler intensities vary). Turn the onions over and broil on the other side until charred, 1 to 2 minutes more. (If you have a charcoal or gas grill, you can grill the onions instead of broiling.) Turn off the broiler and preheat the oven to 400°F.

6 Pour the reserved braising liquid into a measuring cup. You should have about 3 cups; if not, add enough chicken stock to yield 3 cups. Transfer the charred onions to a blender along with the braising liquid, salt, tomatoes, honey, sugar, vinegar, ginger, soy sauce, and chile and blend until the sauce is smooth.

7 Transfer the sauce to a wide, deep skillet or pot and bring it to a simmer over medium-high heat. Reduce the heat to medium and cook, stirring occasionally, until the color of the sauce has deepened and it has thickened to a consistency similar to maple syrup, about 10 minutes.

8 Place the sliced brisket on a rimmed baking sheet and pour some of the sauce over the top. Set the baking sheet in the oven until the brisket is warmed through and the sauce is sizzling, 5 to 7 minutes. Serve with the extra sauce on the side.

heads-up

This recipe calls for 6 hours of braising. On the bright side, the barbecue sauce is pretty quick to make, and the recipe makes a lot of meat!

num pang it

Holy Trinity (page 39), Pickled Asian Pears (page 140), toasted baguette

hoisin meatballs

———

A solid meatball sub (grinder, hero, *num pang* . . .) is a sandwich shop must-have. Of course we wanted ours to reflect the flavors of Southeast Asia, so we added sweet and plummy hoisin sauce, Thai basil, and cooked jasmine rice. For ease of preparation, we bake the meatballs and then finish them low and slow in a big pot of simmering tomatoes. In this recipe, it's particularly important to search out Thai basil instead of standard Italian basil; otherwise, you'll end up with meatballs that taste more like Nonna's rather than *Yeay*'s.

2½ pounds 80% lean ground beef

2 tablespoons kosher salt

2 teaspoons freshly ground
    black pepper

1½ teaspoons sugar

½ cup hoisin sauce

½ cup coarsely chopped fresh Thai
    basil (or Italian basil) leaves, plus
    more for serving

½ cup cooked jasmine rice (page 165)

1 (28-ounce) can whole tomatoes

heads-up

For more caramelized meatballs, panfry them until they are browned on all sides instead of baking them in the oven, then transfer them to the sauce to finish cooking.

num pang it

Holy Trinity (page 39), toasted baguette

1   Preheat the oven to 375°F.

2   Place the ground beef in a large bowl, then add the salt, pepper, sugar, hoisin sauce, basil, and rice. Use your hands to knead the mixture together until everything is well combined. Divide the mixture into golf ball–size portions, rolling each into a nice, round ball (your should have about 24 meatballs).

3   Place the meatballs in a 9 by 13-inch baking dish and bake until browned and cooked through, turning them midway through baking, about 30 minutes.

4   Pour the tomatoes over the meatballs, reduce the oven temperature to 325°F, and continue to cook until the meatballs absorb the flavor of the tomatoes, turn a little red, and are quite soft, about 1½ hours, basting the meatballs occasionally. Remove the meatballs from the oven and let cool in the sauce. Sprinkle more basil over the top and serve.

ad-rock pang

There are three things that people notice when they walk into our shops: people digging our food (naturally), the graffiti, and the music. The sounds tie into our love for Golden Era hip-hop—this is the music closest to our hearts. Ben even saw the Beastie Boys play live in Paris with Run-D.M.C. when he was twelve years old—so when he spotted Ad-Rock from the Beastie Boys at his local NYC dog run, you can bet he didn't let the chance to meet the industry icon slip away. Ben and Ad-Rock bonded over their adopted dogs, and it wasn't long before they started to knock around the idea of an Ad-Rock–Num Pang collaboration. Here it is: the Ad-Rock Pang, a Jewish deli–inspired pastrami sandwich with "Chili Russian" (our chili mayo made with dill pickles and a shot of ketchup) and pickled Kirby cucumbers. The proceeds went to benefit BARC (the Brooklyn Animal Resource Coalition), and the North Shore Animal League, both of which benefit animals in need of finding "forever" homes.

CHILI RUSSIAN DRESSING

1 cup Most Important Chili Mayo (page 40)

¾ teaspoon Worcestershire sauce

½ cup very finely chopped dill pickles, store-bought or homemade (see page 144)

⅓ cup ketchup

1½ teaspoons caraway seeds, toasted (follow the toasted coriander instructions on page 122) and coarsely ground

AD-ROCK PANG

1 pound good-quality Jewish deli–style pastrami

4 (6-inch) baguettes, split lengthwise and toasted

2 medium Kirby cucumbers, thinly sliced lengthwise on an angle into 6 long planks

8 fresh cilantro sprigs

8 fresh dill sprigs

1⅓ cups Holy Pickled Carrots (page 42)

Potato chips (preferably Wise), cream soda, and dill pickle spears, for serving (optional)

1   **MAKE THE CHILI RUSSIAN DRESSING:** In a small bowl, stir together the chili mayo, Worcestershire, pickles, ketchup, and caraway seeds.

2   **MAKE THE AD-ROCK PANG:** Wrap the pastrami in a paper towel and microwave on high in 20-second increments until it is warmed through (or steam the pastrami on the stovetop until it is warmed through).

3   Spread the chili Russian dressing inside each baguette, evenly coating both the top and bottom cut sides. Divide the pastrami among the bottom halves of each baguette. To the top half add a few cucumber slices, followed by 2 cilantro sprigs and 2 dill sprigs. Add the pickled carrots on top, sandwich the two halves together, and serve with potato chips, a cream soda, and a pickle.

grilled skirt steak with crushed coriander and peppercorns

Here, skirt steak gets doused in a peppery-sweet soy glaze that acts like the "glue" for sticking on a generous amount of coarsely crushed coriander seeds—kind of like a Southeast Asian steak au poivre. Coriander is fresh and grassy and the brightness of it works phenomenally with the heat from the pepper. If you can't find skirt steak, you can substitute flank steak instead.

⅓ cup soy sauce

3 tablespoons coarsely ground coriander seeds (preferably freshly ground; see page 122)

2 tablespoons freshly ground black pepper

1½ tablespoons sugar

1½ tablespoons honey

2 pounds skirt steak, cut into 4 pieces

1 tablespoon canola oil

1 In a medium bowl, whisk together the soy sauce, coriander, pepper, sugar, and honey until the sugar has dissolved. Add the steaks to the bowl, turn to coat, and refrigerate for 1 hour.

2 Heat a charcoal or gas grill (or grill pan) to medium-high. Use tongs to dip a folded paper towel in the oil and grease the grill grates. Lay the steaks on the grill and cook without moving them until they are nicely grill marked, 2½ to 3 minutes. Turn the steaks over and cook on the other side until the steaks are cooked to your liking (we cook them to medium-rare), 2½ to 3 minutes more, depending on the thickness of the steak (some pieces may be done before others).

3 Transfer the steaks to a cutting board and let them rest for 5 minutes before slicing into thin pieces crosswise and on an angle. Serve.

num pang it

Holy Trinity (page 39), toasted baguette

KNOW THIS: CRUSHING SPICES

If you don't have a spice grinder or small food processor to pulverize spices, that's no problem. Place the whole spices in a heavy-duty plastic bag, seal, and crush the spices using a heavy pan or soup pot—a rolling pin works, too.

burger pang

There's really no secret to how we end up with what's on our menus. The daily board reflects the food we're into, just with a Num Pang sensibility. We've always wanted to have a burger on the menu, but *everyone* has a burger on their menu . . . the question was how to make ours stand apart from the rest. Turns out, the Southeast Asian profile suits a burger particularly well—add some hoisin sauce to the burger blend, glaze with more hoisin (if it's too thick to brush over the burgers, dilute it with a few drops of vinegar), and top with the Holy Trinity, and you have something truly worthy of waiting on line for. We shape the burger to fit a baguette—but really, a patty would taste just as great if you're serving it tradit-style on a burger bun.

SWEET HOISIN

½ cup hoisin sauce

1 tablespoon ketchup

1¾ teaspoons rice vinegar

1½ teaspoons soy sauce

½ teaspoon cayenne pepper

¼ teaspoon garlic powder

¼ teaspoon grated peeled fresh ginger

¼ teaspoon toasted sesame oil

BURGERS

2½ pounds 80% lean ground chuck

¼ cup cooked jasmine rice (see page 165)

2 tablespoons finely chopped fresh cilantro leaves, plus ½ bunch sprigs

1½ teaspoons kosher salt

1 tablespoon canola oil

½ cup plus 1 tablespoon Most Important Chili Mayo (page 40)

6 (6-inch) baguettes or soft rolls, split lengthwise and toasted

2 cups Holy Pickled Carrots (page 42)

3 medium Kirby cucumbers, thinly sliced lengthwise on an angle into 6 long planks

1 **MAKE THE SWEET HOISIN:** In a medium bowl, whisk together the hoisin sauce, ketchup, vinegar, soy sauce, cayenne, garlic powder, ginger, and oil.

2 **MAKE THE BURGERS:** In a large bowl, combine the ground chuck, jasmine rice, half of the sweet hoisin, the cilantro, and the salt and work together with your hands until well combined. Shape the mixture into cylindrical patties, each about 6 inches long and ½ inch thick.

3 Heat a charcoal or gas grill to high, or heat a grill pan or cast-iron skillet over high heat until very hot. If grilling the burgers, use tongs to dip a folded paper towel into the oil, then use the oiled towel to grease the grill grates. If pan-searing, heat the oil in the pan. Add the burgers and cook until nicely browned, 4 to 6 minutes. Use a spatula to flip the burgers over. Brush the top of each burger with some of the sweet hoisin and cook until the other side is browned, 4 to 5 minutes more for a medium-rare center. Flip the burger again, brush the tops with more sweet hoisin and turn off the heat. Transfer the burgers to a plate and set aside.

4 Divide the chili mayo over the cut sides of each of the baguettes. Set a burger on the bottom baguette half, and divide the cilantro sprigs, pickled carrots, and cucumber slices over each burger. Cover with the top half of the baguette and serve.

new york strip with scallion-chile sauce

If you're looking for a simple way to replicate a steakhouse experience at home, then a boneless New York strip steak is the way to go. Start with your steak at room temperature rather than straight from the fridge—this helps it cook more evenly so you don't have gray edges and a pink center, but rather a rare rosy color all the way through. The sauce is herby and acidic, and is a play on the sauce served with Chinese steamed chicken (it's kind of like a Chinese-style chimichurri).

1 (1½-pound) boneless New York strip steak, 1 inch thick

SCALLION-CHILE SAUCE

16 scallions, green parts only, coarsely chopped

4 large garlic cloves

2 anchovy fillets

Heaping 1 tablespoon coarsely chopped peeled fresh ginger

1 fresh Thai bird's eye chile, coarsely chopped

¾ cup extra-virgin olive oil

1 tablespoon honey

1 tablespoon soy sauce

2 teaspoons kosher salt

1 teaspoon coarsely ground black pepper

1½ tablespoons canola oil

num pang it

Slice the steak very thinly after cooking and place 4 to 6 pieces on each toasted baguette. Cover with the scallion-chile sauce and add Holy Trinity (page 39).

1   Let the steak sit out at room temperature for 45 minutes, then liberally coat both sides of the steak with the salt and pepper, pressing the pepper onto the steak to get it to stick. Set it aside for 15 minutes.

2   **IN THE MEANTIME, MAKE THE SCALLION-CHILE SAUCE:** In a food processor, pulse the scallions, garlic, anchovies, ginger, and chile until fine, about ten 1-second pulses. Add ¼ cup of the oil and process for 5 seconds. Transfer the mixture to a small heat-safe bowl. In a small skillet, heat the remaining ½ cup olive oil over medium-high heat until it begins to smoke, about 3 minutes, then immediately pour it over the scallion mixture. Stir occasionally until the mixture is slightly cooled, then stir in the honey and soy sauce.

3   In a heavy-bottomed medium skillet (cast iron is great), heat the oil over high heat until it begins to smoke, 3 to 4 minutes (open the windows—things are going to get smoky). Add the steak (set the tip of the steak in the pan first, then lay the steak down going away from you so the hot oil doesn't spatter up and burn you), and reduce the heat to medium-high.

4   Let the steak brown for 4 minutes, then turn it over onto the skinny, fatty edge and brown the edge, about 4 minutes (you'll have to hold it with tongs until it is browned). Turn the steak over to caramelize the other edge, about 1 minute, then discard all but 1 to 2 tablespoons of fat from the skillet. Turn the steak onto the uncooked flat side to brown it, about 2 minutes for rare. Transfer the steak to a wire rack to rest for 8 minutes, then set it on a cutting board and slice crosswise and against the grain into ¼-inch-thick pieces. Serve drizzled with the scallion-chile sauce.

braised short ribs and vinegary scallions with cauliflower puree

---

Watching Ratha cook is like watching a mad scientist in a lab—pinches of this, a splash of that—turn your back for a minute and when you look in the pot it's like pure alchemy bubbling in a cauldron. Ratha never trained at culinary school or as a line cook—he learned by eating. This dish is an homage to a chef Ratha worked with, Cyril Renaud of the now closed Fleur de Sel in New York City. While the robust braised short ribs definitely have their roots in France, they get their distinct Southeast Asian feel thanks to the soy sauce and tangy scallion finish.

SHORT RIBS

4 meaty English-cut short ribs (about 4 pounds)

10 large garlic cloves: 4 finely chopped, 6 left whole

1 medium yellow onion, ½ sliced into thick rings, the other half finely chopped

3 teaspoons kosher salt, plus more as needed

1 fresh rosemary sprig

3 tablespoons extra-virgin olive oil

½ teaspoon sugar

1 (28-ounce) can crushed tomatoes

½ cup soy sauce

3 tablespoons honey

2 tablespoons apple cider vinegar

½ teaspoon red pepper flakes

⅛ teaspoon ground coriander (preferably freshly ground; see page 122)

⅛ teaspoon ground ginger

2 tablespoons red wine

1   **MAKE THE SHORT RIBS:** Place the short ribs, fatty-side down, in a large pot over medium-high heat and cook until the fat begins to render, 2 to 3 minutes.

2   Set the pot slightly askew over the burner and add the whole garlic cloves to the cooler side of the pot that is not directly over the heat (so they don't get too dark). Cook the short ribs until they are browned on all sides, 8 to 10 minutes.

3   Add the onion rings, 2 teaspoons of the salt, and enough water to come halfway up the sides of the short ribs. Add the rosemary, bring the water to a simmer, then reduce the heat to medium-low. Partially cover the pot and cook the short ribs until the liquid has reduced by about half, 1 to 1½ hours (the liquid should be at a bare simmer—one or two bubbles occasionally popping at the surface—cook over low heat if necessary).

4   Meanwhile, in a large skillet, heat the oil over medium-high heat until it shimmers, about 2 minutes. Add the chopped onion, reduce the heat to medium, and cook, stirring often, until the onion starts to soften and become transparent, 3 to 4 minutes. Stir in the chopped garlic, the remaining teaspoon of salt, and the sugar and cook until the garlic is fragrant, about 1 minute. Add the tomatoes, reduce the heat to medium-low, and cook, stirring occasionally, until the oil pools on the surface of the tomatoes, 15 to 20 minutes. Turn off the heat, taste, and adjust with more salt if needed. Set ½ cup aside and refrigerate the rest for another time.

CAULIFLOWER PUREE

1 large head cauliflower (about
   3 pounds), cored and cut into
   2-inch pieces

1 tablespoon plus ¼ teaspoon kosher
   salt, plus more as needed

1 cup whole milk, warmed

1½ sticks (6 ounces) unsalted butter,
   at room temperature

½ cup crumbled feta cheese

½ teaspoon sugar

VINEGARY SCALLIONS

2 teaspoons canola oil

6 scallions, halved crosswise

¼ teaspoon kosher salt

¼ teaspoon freshly ground
   black pepper

Pinch of sugar

2 teaspoons apple cider vinegar

heads-up

The short ribs braise for a few hours.
Be prepared for your house to smell
amazing.

num pang it

Pull the meat off the short rib bones.
Instead of using the cauliflower puree,
use the roasted cauliflower on page
128 (for texture). Pile the meat and
cauliflower on a toasted baguette. Top
with the vinegary scallions and Holy
Trinity (page 39).

5   Add the reserved ½ cup tomato sauce, the soy sauce, honey, vinegar, the red pepper flakes, coriander, and ginger to the short ribs. Return to a simmer over medium-high heat, then reduce the heat to medium-low and continue to simmer until a fork easily slides into the meat without resistance, 1½ to 2 hours more (add a splash of water every now and then if the liquid becomes too thick). Add the wine, cook for 5 minutes more, and turn off the heat.

6   **WHILE THE SHORT RIBS SIMMER, MAKE THE CAULIFLOWER PUREE:** Bring a large pot of water to a boil over high heat. Add the cauliflower and 1 tablespoon of the salt and cook until a fork easily slides into the cauliflower, about 6 minutes. Drain the cauliflower and transfer it to a food processor or blender. Add the milk, butter, feta, sugar, and remaining ¼ teaspoon salt. Process the cauliflower until it is creamy and smooth; taste and adjust the salt if needed.

7   **MAKE THE VINEGARY SCALLIONS:** Heat a medium skillet over medium-high heat. Add the oil, scallions, salt, pepper, and sugar. Cook, shaking the pan occasionally, until the scallions start to blister, 2 to 3 minutes. Pour the vinegar over the scallions, shake to distribute, and turn off the heat.

8   Divide the cauliflower among four plates. Set a short rib over the cauliflower with plenty of sauce, then add a scallion on top.

lemongrass leg of lamb

A gently sautéed lemongrass-and-shallot paste works triple time on this boneless leg of lamb roast: once as a wet rub for the interior of the roast, once as an herb paste for the exterior, and finally as a sauce to serve alongside the finished roast. The taste of the rub is really robust from a small mountain of shallots and garlic, but the bite is tempered by a few cups of fresh mint and herbaceous lemongrass. When you ask for the butterflied leg of lamb roast from the butcher, ask for a thin layer of fat to be left on the surface and for all the pockets of fat to be trimmed from the interior of the roast.

½ cup extra-virgin olive oil

15 medium shallots, finely chopped

18 garlic cloves, finely chopped, plus
    4 garlic cloves, halved lengthwise

6 lemongrass stalks, tough outer
    layers removed, tender reed
    finely chopped

3 cups fresh mint leaves, coarsely
    chopped

1 boneless butterflied leg of lamb
    (about 5 pounds), untied (if tied into
    a roast) and silverskin removed

1½ tablespoons kosher salt

1 tablespoon freshly ground
    black pepper

1 In a medium saucepan, heat the oil over medium heat until it shimmers. Add the shallots and sweat them, stirring often, until they become translucent, about 6 minutes (if the shallots start to brown, reduce the heat to medium-low). Stir in the garlic and cook until it is fragrant and soft, about 2 minutes (don't brown the garlic). Stir in the lemongrass and mint and turn off the heat. Transfer the mixture to a heat-safe bowl and set aside to cool to room temperature.

2 Place the lamb on a cutting board, fat-side down. Season with half the salt and half the pepper, then spread half the cooled lemongrass-shallot mixture over the lamb and use your hands to massage it in. Roll the lamb into one long roast and use butcher's twine to secure it at 1½ to 2-inch intervals. Season the exterior of the roast with the remaining salt and pepper, then massage half the remaining lemongrass-shallot mixture onto the exterior of the roast. Place the lamb on a roasting rack set into a roasting pan and set aside at room temperature. Meanwhile, preheat the oven to 275°F.

3 Roast the lamb until an instant-read thermometer inserted into the thickest part registers 130°F to 135°F, about 2 hours. Remove the roasting pan from the oven (leave the lamb on the rack in the pan) and loosely tent the lamb with aluminum foil. Set the roast aside for 20 minutes to rest.

heads-up

Open a nice bottle of red and settle in while the lamb roasts good and slow for up to 2 hours.

num pang it

Slice the lamb very thinly after cooking and place 4 to 6 pieces on a toasted baguette. Add 2 tablespoons of chopped mint to Chili Yogurt (page 40) and spread it over the inside of the baguette. Add Holy Trinity (page 39) and serve.

4 When you're ready to serve, preheat the oven temperature to 500°F. Return the lamb to the oven and roast it for 15 minutes to rewarm and get an extra-nice degree of caramelization on the surface. Transfer the roast to a carving board, remove the twine, and carve the roast crosswise into ¼- to ½-inch-thick slices. Serve with the remaining lemongrass-shallot mixture.

FISH & SHELLFISH

BLUEFISH ESCABECHE WITH BLOOD ORANGES
    AND CHILES 107

PEPPERCORN CATFISH 111

CRISPY FISH CAKES WITH CHILI MAYO 112

GRILLED MAHI-MAHI WITH SAUTÉED LEEKS 114

SEARED COCONUT TIGER SHRIMP 117

PAN-ROASTED SALMON, GINGER-BEET PICKLE, AND SPICY
    DILL YOGURT 118

CORIANDER-AND-PEPPERCORN-CRUSTED TUNA WITH
    BLACK OLIVE RELISH 121

NUM PANG LOBSTER ROLL 123

bluefish escabeche with blood oranges and chiles

We tap into an old-school cooking method here to cure parcooked fish in an assertively flavored marinade for twenty-four hours in the fridge before serving. Escabeche needs to be made with a strong-flavored fish like bluefish that can stand up to the pickling liquid—ours is loaded with blood orange, coriander, garlic, bay leaves, jalapeño, and lemon. This is a beautiful dish to keep in your fridge during the summertime. Since it is "pickled," it doesn't have to be reheated or anything before serving. Pack it in a mason jar and bring it to a picnic or grill-out to really impress your host. Here along the Northeast Corridor, bluefish and summer go together like the Fourth of July and fireworks. If you don't have bluefish where you live, substitute any strong-flavored fish, such as mackerel, sardines, or tuna.

BLUEFISH

1 (12-ounce) bluefish fillet

1 teaspoon kosher salt

½ teaspoon ground black pepper

2 tablespoons Wondra, cake, or all-purpose flour (see page 120)

1 tablespoon canola oil

ESCABECHE

½ large red onion, thinly sliced

4 thinly sliced lemon rounds

4 thinly sliced blood orange rounds

4 garlic cloves, smashed

2 fresh bay leaves

1½ teaspoons whole coriander seeds

1½ teaspoons yellow mustard seeds

2 tablespoons drained brine-packed capers

1 small jalapeño, halved lengthwise and thinly sliced into strips

1 fresh red chile, halved lengthwise and thinly sliced into strips

3 tablespoons apple cider vinegar

2 tablespoons kosher salt

2 teaspoons sugar

1 cup fresh cilantro (with stems)

½ cup Chili Yogurt (page 40), for serving

1 **MAKE THE BLUEFISH:** Place the bluefish fillet skin-side up on a cutting board. Using a sharp knife, make a few very shallow slashes in the skin that are about 1 inch long and just deep enough to penetrate the skin without cutting into the flesh (this is to ensure the fillets stay flat when pan-searing). Season both sides of the fillet with salt and pepper and then sprinkle the flour over both sides of the fillet, gently patting the flour so it sticks.

2 In a medium skillet, heat the oil over medium-high heat. Once it starts to smoke, add the fish skin-side down and cook until it is just becoming golden brown, about 3 minutes. Use a spatula to flip the fish and cook on the other side until it starts to color, 2 to 3 minutes more. Transfer the fillet to a large plate and set aside to cool to room temperature. Gently peel away and discard the skin and place the fish in a deep container.

3 **MAKE THE ESCABECHE:** Reduce the heat to medium and add the onion to one side of the skillet and the lemon and orange rounds to the other, making sure they lie flat so they can brown evenly. Add the garlic cloves over the onions, then add the bay leaves on top. Sprinkle the coriander and mustard seeds over the onions and cook until the citrus rounds begin to brown, 3 to 4 minutes. Turn the rounds over and cook on the other side until browned, 1 to 2 minutes more, then stir everything together. Add the capers, jalapeño, and chile and cook for 1 minute more.

recipe continues

4   While the onions and aromatics cook, in a medium bowl, whisk together the vinegar, salt, sugar, and 1½ cups water. Add the liquid to the onion mixture, raise the heat to high, and bring everything to a boil. Turn off the heat and add the cilantro. Transfer the curing liquid to a heat-safe bowl to cool to room temperature, then pour the brine over the fish, cover the container, and refrigerate for 24 hours (or up to 1 week).

5   To serve, remove the fish from the brine and slice it crosswise into four pieces. Serve drizzled with the brine and a spoonful of chili yogurt in top.

heads-up

The fish takes 24 hours to pickle and keeps for up to 4 days in the fridge.

num pang it

Holy Trinity (page 39), toasted baguette

peppercorn catfish

Inspired by a sweet-and-spicy clay-pot catfish dish that Ratha's mom makes, the peppercorn catfish *num pang* has surprisingly become one of Num Pang's most popular sandwiches. Our version is pan-seared, then finished with a peppery soy-honey glaze. The catfish takes on a killer sweet-and-spicy taste that is amazing in a sandwich or simply served alongside steamed white rice with some kind of pickle to offset the sharpness of the sauce. You might have some of the peppercorn sauce leftover—it's great drizzled over pan-seared chicken or tossed into fried rice or a stir-fry.

PEPPERCORN GLAZE

1 cup soy sauce

½ cup honey

¼ cup distilled white vinegar

2 tablespoons kosher salt

1½ tablespoons sugar

3 tablespoons freshly ground black pepper

1 (1-inch) piece fresh ginger, peeled and thinly sliced into matchsticks

CATFISH

4 (8-ounce) catfish fillets

1 tablespoon plus 1½ teaspoons freshly ground black pepper

½ teaspoon kosher salt

1 tablespoon canola oil

5 scallions, white and light green parts only, finely chopped

heads-up

A coffee grinder makes quick work of finely pulverizing the peppercorns. If, after tasting the sauce, you find it is too peppery and intense (lightweight!), strain out the peppercorns (the sauce will still have plenty of heat).

num pang it

Holy Trinity (page 39), toasted baguette

1   **MAKE THE PEPPERCORN GLAZE:** In a medium saucepan, combine the soy sauce, honey, vinegar, salt, and sugar. Stir to combine, then bring the mixture to a boil over medium-high heat. Reduce the heat to medium-low and simmer until the mixture has reduced by about half, 10 to 12 minutes. Stir in the pepper and ginger, cook for 30 seconds, then turn off the heat. Once it cools, it will be about the consistency of maple syrup.

2   **MAKE THE CATFISH:** Season both sides of the catfish fillets with 1½ teaspoons of the pepper and the salt. In a large nonstick skillet, heat the oil over medium-high heat. Place the catfish fillets in the skillet and cook until browned, 4 to 5 minutes. Gently turn the fillets over and cook on the other side for 2 minutes, then add ½ cup of the glaze.

3   Continue to cook, basting the fish with the glaze often, until the thickest part of the fillet feels firm to gentle pressure and the glaze is bubbling, 2 to 3 minutes. Sprinkle with some or all of the remaining 1 tablespoon pepper, if desired.

4   Transfer each fillet to a plate and serve with sauce drizzled over the top and sprinkled with the scallions.

crispy fish cakes with chili mayo

If you're a fan of crab cakes or salmon cakes, make these. Like right now. Taking a bite is like digging into the best hits of Asia: the crunch of panko bread crumbs, the freshness of cilantro, the sharpness of scallions, garlic, and ginger . . . you kind of can't go wrong. We use catfish fillets but really any medium- to firm-fleshed fish will do, like haddock or even tilapia. In this recipe, it's important to keep everything cold. It keeps the protein in the fish firm and the cilantro bright and green.

1¾ pounds boneless, skinless catfish fillets, chopped into 2-inch pieces

1 cup chopped fresh cilantro leaves

4 scallions, finely chopped

2 garlic cloves, finely chopped

1½ tablespoons finely chopped peeled fresh ginger

1½ tablespoons toasted sesame oil

1 tablespoon plus 1 teaspoon ground toasted coriander seeds (preferably freshly ground; see page 122)

1 tablespoon cornstarch

Grated zest of 1 lime

1 teaspoon ground dried Thai bird's eye chile or cayenne pepper

1 large egg

½ teaspoon kosher salt

2¼ cups panko bread crumbs

¼ cup canola oil

Most Important Chili Mayo (page 40)

Thai basil, for serving (optional)

heads-up

The fish cake mixture needs to chill for 30 minutes before shaping.

num pang it

Holy Trinity (page 39), toasted baguette

1   Place the bowl and blade for a food processor in the freezer to chill while you prep the rest of the ingredients.

2   In a food processor bowl, combine the fish, cilantro, scallions, garlic, ginger, sesame oil, coriander, cornstarch, lime zest, chile, egg, and salt. Process the mixture, scraping down the sides of the bowl after 4 to 5 seconds, until it is semismooth with some chunky bits, about 12 seconds total. Transfer the mixture to a medium bowl and stir in ¾ cup of the bread crumbs. Cover the fish mixture with a piece of plastic wrap and place it in the freezer until well chilled, 15 to 20 minutes.

3   Preheat the oven to 375°F.

4   Put the remaining 1½ cups bread crumbs in a shallow dish. Divide the chilled fish mixture into six ¾-inch-thick cakes and press both sides of each fish cake into the bread crumbs.

5   In a large oven-safe nonstick skillet, heat the canola oil for 2 minutes over medium heat. Add a fish cake—bubbles should immediately surround the fish cake (if there aren't any bubbles, heat the oil a bit longer). Add the remaining fish cakes and cook until both sides are golden, 1 to 2 minutes per side. Transfer the skillet to the oven and finish cooking the fish cakes until they are cooked through, 4 to 5 minutes (you can also finish the fish cakes on a baking sheet if your skillet isn't oven-safe). Remove from the oven and serve with lots of chili mayo for dipping, and sprinkled with Thai basil (if using).

grilled mahi-mahi with sautéed leeks

In many ways, we have to be as nimble about our seafood choices as a home cook. If no one is catching any mahi-mahi, then two things can happen: the price for what is available at the market skyrockets, *or*, plain and simple, there is no mahi-mahi. So we do what you'd do at the store: pick another fish. Sometimes you'll see this combination on our menu with Spanish mackerel, an oily and strong-flavored fish that takes beautifully to the intensely herbaceous and slightly spicy marinade. We've also made this *pang* with local bluefish, which is similar in flavor and texture to mackerel. Mahi-mahi is probably the tamest-tasting fish, but its steak-y texture just rocks this sandwich. When salmon is plentiful, it's beautiful marinated and grilled, too . . . so pick what looks best, then go for it.

MAHI-MAHI

1 cup fresh Thai basil leaves

½ cup fresh cilantro leaves

½ cup canola oil

¼ cup fresh lime juice

¼ cup apple cider vinegar

1 garlic clove, coarsely chopped

¼ jalapeño, coarsely chopped

1 teaspoon kosher salt

½ teaspoon freshly ground
    black pepper

4 (6- to 8-ounce) mahi-mahi fillets

SAUTÉED LEEKS

1 tablespoon canola oil

4 medium leeks, white and light
    green parts only, halved lengthwise
    and thinly sliced crosswise

½ teaspoon kosher salt

¼ teaspoon freshly ground
    black pepper

1 tablespoon canola oil, for grilling

Coarsely chopped fresh cilantro, for
    serving

num pang it

Holy Trinity (page 39), toasted baguette

1 **MARINATE THE MAHI-MAHI:** In a blender, combine the basil, cilantro, oil, lime juice, vinegar, garlic, jalapeño, salt, and pepper and blend until completely smooth. Set the fish in an airtight container and pour the marinade over the top. Cover and refrigerate for at least 6 hours and up to 12 hours.

2 **MAKE THE LEEKS:** In a large skillet, heat the oil over medium-high heat until it shimmers, about 2 minutes. Add the leeks, salt, and pepper, reduce the heat to medium, and cook, stirring often, until the leeks are soft but not browned, 4 to 5 minutes.

3 Heat a charcoal or gas grill to high, or heat a grill pan over high heat. Remove the fish from the marinade and blot dry with paper towels. Dip a folded paper towel into the oil and use tongs and the oiled paper towel to grease the grill grates. Set the fish on top and grill until marked and golden brown, 3 to 4 minutes. Turn the fish over and grill on the other side until the flesh is grill marked and the center of the fillet resists light pressure, 3 to 4 minutes more.

4 Serve the mahi-mahi with the leeks on top and sprinkled with cilantro.

heads-up

This fish needs to marinate for at least 6 hours before grilling.

It goes without saying to only buy the best-quality fish you can find. It should smell fresh and sweet—if there is any trace of fishiness, just walk away. And by the way, there's nothing wrong with buying frozen fish—it's often fresher than "fresh" since it hasn't been sitting out exposed to oxygen and under lights at the grocery store. Defrost it overnight in the fridge or place the sealed package under cold, running water for about 20 minutes to thaw (maybe longer if it's something extra thick, like a tuna steak). We like to bring steaks—be they fish, beef, or pork—to room temperature before cooking so they'll cook more quickly and evenly. Unlike steaks and roasts, though, fish doesn't need to rest before serving.

seared coconut tiger shrimp

Sweet shrimp quickly seared on the flattop then tossed with coconut milk and shredded coconut . . . what's not to like? This is one of our most popular sandwiches, but stripped of the bread, it becomes a great on its own, whether served over plain or "basic" rice (page 165), noodles, or even toasted bread. We like tiger shrimp because they have a lobster-like texture and incredibly sweet flavor—search them out and you'll be happy (if you can't find them, buy sweet white shrimp instead).

1 tablespoon canola oil

1 pound (21 to 25 count) shrimp (preferably tiger shrimp), peeled and deveined

1 teaspoon kosher salt, plus more as needed

½ teaspoon freshly ground black pepper

¾ cup coconut milk

1 tablespoon unsweetened desiccated coconut, toasted

num pang it

Holy Trinity (page 39), toasted baguette

1   Heat a large skillet over high heat for 2 minutes, add the oil, and once it shimmers, add the shrimp. Season the shrimp with the salt and pepper and cook until they start to turn opaque around the edges but are still raw in the center, about 1 minute.

2   Turn the shrimp over and add the coconut milk. Cook briefly on the other side just until the shrimp are cooked through, about 1 minute more. Transfer to a bowl and season with more salt (if needed) and serve sprinkled with the coconut.

pan-roasted salmon, ginger-beet pickle, and spicy dill yogurt

Salmon, beets, dill, and ginger: this dish is a total mishmash of both our cultures and backgrounds. In a nod to Southeast Asia, we add pickled ginger to Eastern European–style pickled beets just before serving (if you mix the beets and ginger, the ginger will turn pink—not that there is anything wrong with that, we just like the color contrast of the two when kept separate), and use our Chili Yogurt (page 40) as the foundation for the fresh dill-yogurt sauce. Because of the way salmon is structured, especially wild salmon that can be a bit thinner than farmed salmon, if using wild salmon we pan-sear two larger pieces rather than four long and skinny cross-sections from the belly of the fish.

PICKLE

1 (2-inch) piece fresh ginger, peeled

1 medium beet, peeled

2 cups apple cider vinegar

2 tablespoons whole coriander seeds

2 tablespoons fennel seeds

2 tablespoons sugar

1 tablespoon whole black peppercorns

1 small dried red chile

1 teaspoon kosher salt

SALMON

2 (10- to 12-ounce) skin-on wild salmon fillets, or 4 (5- to 6-ounce farmed salmon fillets

1½ teaspoons kosher salt

1 teaspoon freshly ground black pepper

2 tablespoons Wondra flour, cake flour, or all-purpose flour (see page 120)

1 tablespoon canola oil

2 cups Chili Yogurt (page 40)

½ cup finely chopped fresh dill

1   **MAKE THE PICKLE:** Fill a small bowl with ice and water and set aside. Using a mandoline (or a sharp chef's knife), slice the ginger very thin (not paper-thin—you want the pickle to have some texture), stack the slices, then use a chef's knife to slice them lengthwise into thin matchsticks. Bring a small saucepan of water to a boil, add the ginger, and blanch for 30 seconds. Drain and shock in the ice water, then drain the ginger and place it in a heat-safe container. Slice the beet into matchsticks in the same manner, and place it in a separate heat-safe container.

2   Combine the vinegar, coriander, fennel, sugar, peppercorns, chile, salt, and 1 cup water in a medium saucepan and bring to a simmer over medium-high heat. Reduce the heat to medium-low and gently simmer for 5 minutes. Strain half the liquid through a fine-mesh sieve over the ginger; strain the remaining liquid through the sieve over the beets. Let cool to room temperature, then cover and refrigerate for at least 2 hours or up to 2 weeks.

recipe continues

The pickle needs at least a few hours to pickle in the fridge and is best if made at least 1 day ahead of serving.

num pang it

Holy Trinity (page 39; substituting the dill-enhanced chili yogurt for straight-up chili mayo), toasted baguette

KNOW THIS: THE SECRET TO CRISPY FISH SKIN

Dusting fish skin with a low-protein "instant" flour is the secret to getting a crackling-crisp skin on fish fillets or even skin-on pan-seared chicken. We use Wondra flour since its available in most supermarkets. If you don't have any in the house, the next best substitute is cake flour, and if you don't have that, go ahead and use all-purpose. You can also use instant flour to thicken sauces without dissolving it in water first (unlike cornstarch), making it a secret weapon in many restaurant kitchens.

3   **MAKE THE SALMON:** Place the salmon fillets skin-side up on a cutting board. Using a sharp knife, make a few very shallow slashes in the skin that are about 1 inch long and just deep enough to penetrate the skin without cutting into the flesh (this is to ensure the fillets stay flat when pan-searing). Season the skin side with salt and pepper and then sprinkle 1 tablespoon of the flour over each fillet, gently patting the flour onto the skin. Turn the fillets over and season the flesh with the remaining salt and pepper.

4   Heat the oil in a medium skillet over medium-high heat. Once the oil gets very hot and shimmers (but before it starts to smoke), add the salmon to the skillet, skin-side down. Reduce the heat to medium and cook, without moving, until the skin is deeply golden brown, about 6 minutes. Use a spatula to gently flip the fillets and cook on the other side until the thickest part of the fillet resists light pressure and the edges are slightly more firm, about 3 minutes for rare. Transfer the fillets to a cutting board and slice each in half.

5   Stir together the chili yogurt and dill. Serve each piece of salmon topped with some pickled beets and ginger and with a generous spoonful of the dill yogurt.

coriander-and-peppercorn-crusted tuna with black olive relish

People think that as restaurateurs, we never have time to cook at home, but that's so incredibly untrue! We cook all the time—for our friends, family, or for ourselves on a quiet Sunday night. This dish is a perfect example of what we make. Big on flavor, easy on prep, fast on time. Our flagship store in the NoMad area of Manhattan is close to a great fish market, and sometimes before or after work we'll pick up some tuna, salmon, or smelt and go to town.

BLACK OLIVE RELISH

1 large shallot, coarsely chopped

Heaping 1 tablespoon coarsely chopped peeled fresh ginger

½ cup pitted Niçoise olives

½ cup pitted Kalamata olives

½ cup Pickled Red Cabbage (page 142)

½ cup extra-virgin olive oil

3 tablespoons apple cider vinegar

3 tablespoons coarsely chopped fresh cilantro leaves

TUNA

2 (8- to 10-ounce) tuna steaks

1 tablespoon extra-virgin olive oil

2 teaspoons kosher salt

¼ cup coarsely ground coriander (preferably freshly ground; see page 122)

¼ cup freshly ground black pepper

2 tablespoons canola oil

1   **MAKE THE BLACK OLIVE RELISH:** In a food processor, combine the shallot and ginger and pulse until finely chopped. Add the olives, cabbage, oil, vinegar, and cilantro and pulse until well combined (don't puree—you want a coarse texture). Transfer to a medium bowl and set aside.

2   **MAKE THE TUNA:** Set the tuna on a large plate and rub each fillet with the olive oil, making sure to coat the edges as well as the top and bottom. Rub each fillet with salt (getting the edges, too). Combine the coriander with the pepper, then rub the spice blend over each fillet, making sure to get the edges, too, and firmly patting it on so the spices stick. Set aside for 20 minutes to come to room temperature.

3   Heat a medium skillet over high heat for 2 minutes. Add the canola oil and once it starts to smoke, after 1 to 2 minutes, add the tuna steaks. Let the fish cook, without moving, until it is nicely golden brown, 3 to 4 minutes. Use tongs to turn one fillet over to sear the other side. Hold the other fillet on its side so the edges sear. Once all the edges are browned, turn the tuna to its uncooked side and repeat the searing with the other tuna fillet. You want to make sure your skillet stays searing hot so the spices brown and the tuna doesn't overcook and still gives to light pressure, about 8 minutes total.

recipe continues

We add our Pickled Red Cabbage (page 142) to the relish for more texture and crunch—but if you don't have a walk-in fridge with several tubs of pickled cabbage handy, sub in very thinly sliced raw cabbage. It will essentially pickle while it marinates with the other ingredients, and you'll end up in just about the same place.

num pang it

Black Olive Relish (page 121), Holy Trinity (page 39), toasted baguette

4   Transfer the tuna to a cutting board and slice it crosswise into ½-inch pieces. Divide the tuna among individual plates and serve topped with the relish.

KNOW THIS: TOAST AND GRIND YOUR OWN CORIANDER

Know why you should grind your own coriander? Because it tastes infinitely better, fresher, and more citrusy than the store-bought preground stuff. It takes seconds with a coffee grinder—just add the whole coriander seeds to the coffee grinder and pulse until they're coarsely ground (you want about 30 percent of the coriander seeds to still look kind of seedy). Store in a glass jar in a cool, dark spot for up to 6 months for best flavor.

For an extra layer of flavor, toast the whole coriander seeds in a dry skillet for 2 to 3 minutes, or until they smell fragrant. Let cool on a plate, then grind as above. (Note that toasted spices generally last about half as long as spices in the raw.) If you're exposing a vegetable or protein to direct heat (like a grill or broiler), then don't use toasted coriander, because the spice is more likely to burn.

num pang lobster roll

Ben has a special relationship with lobsters. For the first four years of his culinary career, he literally was responsible for cooking and breaking down anywhere from thirty to eighty lobsters a day. Even though he couldn't look at a lobster for a long, *long* time, he is still as obsessed with a lobster-packed lobster roll as anyone else—except that his has to have Num Pang's signature special blend of flavor and crunch. So we poach the lobster in a gingery court bouillon, then combine the cooked and spice-infused lobster with red bell peppers, Thai basil, scallion, and lemongrass, and top it with our Holy Trinity of Num Pang–ness—cilantro, cukes, chile mayo, and of course pickled carrots.

LOBSTER

1 (4-inch) piece fresh ginger, sliced lengthwise into ¼-inch-thick pieces (no need to peel)

4 fresh tarragon sprigs

2 tablespoons whole black peppercorns

2 tablespoons whole coriander seeds

1 lemongrass stalk, tough outer layer removed, tender stalk bruised with the back of a knife

Splash of apple cider vinegar

2 (1¼-pound) live lobsters

1   **MAKE THE LOBSTER:** Fill a large, deep pot (a lobster pot, stockpot, or canning pot all work well) two-thirds full with water. Add the ginger, tarragon, peppercorns, coriander, lemongrass, and vinegar and bring the mixture to a simmer over medium-high heat.

2   Fill a large bowl with ice and water and set aside. Set the lobsters on a cutting board, making sure the rubber bands are securing their claws. Working with one lobster at a time, place the tip of a sharp chef's knife above the head, just where the head meets the body (there is a natural X right at that spot—aim the tip of the knife at the center of the X), then quickly and with force slice down through the head (this kills the lobster immediately, even though its legs and claws might be wriggling). Repeat with the other lobster.

3   Add the lobsters to the poaching liquid, reduce the heat to medium-low, and cook until the small "thumb" of the claw can be easily pulled off, 10 to 11 minutes. Use tongs or a slotted spoon to immediately transfer the lobsters to the ice water bath. Chill until cool enough to handle, 3 to 5 minutes.

recipe continues

LOBSTER ROLL

3 tablespoons Most Important Chili Mayo (page 40)

1 medium red bell pepper, seeded and finely chopped

2 scallions, green parts only, thinly sliced

2 fresh tarragon sprigs, plus 1 teaspoon finely chopped fresh tarragon leaves

½ teaspoon finely chopped lemongrass (the tender inner stalk)

¼ teaspoon kosher salt

¼ teaspoon freshly ground black pepper

2 (6-inch baguettes), split lengthwise and toasted

⅔ cup Holy Pickled Carrots (page 42)

8 fresh cilantro sprigs

1 medium Kirby cucumber, thinly sliced lengthwise on an angle into 6 long planks

4   **MAKE THE LOBSTER ROLL:** Remove the lobster meat from the tails and claws and chop it into large, bite-size pieces. In a large bowl, stir together 2 tablespoons of the chili mayo, the bell pepper, scallions, chopped tarragon leaves, chopped lemongrass, salt, and black pepper. Stir to combine, then add the lobster meat and gently toss to combine.

5   Divide the remaining 1 tablespoon chili mayo among the top half of each of the baguettes. Divide the lobster salad among the bottom half of the baguettes, then top with the pickled carrots, cilantro and tarragon sprigs, and 3 cucumber slices per sandwich. Cover with the top half of the baguettes and serve.

heads-up

If killing lobsters makes you squeamish (yes, the most humane way is to slice straight through its brain), sub 1 pound of raw peel-on shrimp poached in the court bouillon. Once the shrimp start to curl, transfer to an ice bath, peel and devein, then proceed. Adding a little vinegar to the lobster poaching liquid is the trick to make the lobster meat a lot easier to remove from the shell.

VEG

BEET-MARINATED GRILLED PORTOBELLOS 127

ROASTED CAULIFLOWER WITH THAI EGGPLANT PUREE 128

SALT-AND-PEPPER YAMS WITH SWISS CHARD 131

SPICY GLAZED TOFU 132

beet-marinated grilled portobellos

If a sandwich shop is going to offer a vegetarian sandwich, the culinary hive mind has to at least consider portobello mushrooms as an option. Our challenge—how to improve upon the portobello sandwich and make it, well, interesting? Answer: Roasted. Beet. Marinade. It's sweet, it's pretty, and it adds loads of vitamins, minerals, and even umami to the mushroom. It's unique, and really, we think it makes our portobello mushroom *pang* one of the most creative and delicious mushroom sandwiches around.

BEET MARINADE

3 medium beets, scrubbed well

2 tablespoons canola oil

2 tablespoons kosher salt

1 tablespoon ground black pepper

¾ cup fresh cilantro leaves

¼ cup extra-virgin olive oil

1 tablespoon apple cider vinegar

1 tablespoon honey

½ teaspoon sugar

½ teaspoon ground dried red chile

GRILLED PORTOBELLOS

6 large portobello mushrooms, stemmed

1½ tablespoons canola oil

1 teaspoon kosher salt

½ teaspoon freshly ground black pepper

heads-up

Substitute store-bought roasted beets to save a step; you'll still need at least 4 hours to marinate the mushrooms (no shortcuts here, please!).

num pang it

Holy Trinity (page 39; use the Chili-Soy Mayo), ½ cup Swiss chard (page 131; use about 2 tablespoons per sandwich), toasted baguette

1. **MAKE THE BEET MARINADE:** Preheat the oven to 375°F. Toss the beets in a medium bowl with the canola oil, 1 tablespoon of the salt, and 1½ teaspoons of the pepper. Wrap each beet in aluminum foil so it is completely enclosed. Roast the beets on a rimmed baking sheet until a paring knife easily slides into the center of the largest beet, about 1 hour. Remove the beets from the oven and set them aside until they are cool enough to handle, about 15 minutes. Use a paper towel to rub the skin off of the beets, then quarter each one.

2. Transfer the beets to a blender along with the cilantro, olive oil, vinegar, honey, sugar, chile, remaining salt and pepper, and ½ cup water and blend until well combined (the consistency should be about as thick as tomato juice). Set aside until ready to use.

3. **GRILL THE PORTOBELLOS:** Heat a grill pan over medium-high heat or a charcoal or gas grill to medium-high. Brush both sides of each mushroom with oil, then sprinkle with salt and pepper. Grill the mushrooms until both sides have grill marks, about 3 minutes total. Transfer the mushrooms to a cutting board and slice each in half, then place them in a gallon-size resealable plastic bag. Pour the marinade over the mushrooms, seal the bag, and refrigerate for 1 to 2 hours.

4. Preheat the oven to 400°F. Place the mushrooms in a baking dish or on a rimmed sheet pan, cap-side down, and drizzle each with a spoonful of the marinade. Bake the mushrooms just until they are warmed through, 8 to 10 minutes. Serve hot.

roasted cauliflower with thai eggplant puree

When we first set out to create the Num Pang menu, it was incredibly important to us to create interesting vegetarian and vegan options that would satisfy even the most die-hard carnivore (like the two of us). We can confirm that this sandwich does just that. The eggplant puree is incredibly savory and creamy while the cauliflower adds a good, toothsome bite. Chinese eggplants are long and slender with tender pale-purple skin; small and round Thai eggplants are white with faint green stripes. You may be tempted to rule out hunting down these two varieties, but we encourage you to at least try to find them, as their uniqueness when used in combination is part of the reason the flavor of the eggplant puree is so deeply satisfying. If you can't find Thai eggplants, use all Chinese eggplants.

⅓ cup tomato paste

2 teaspoons kosher salt, plus more as needed

1 teaspoon freshly ground black pepper, plus more as needed

1½ pounds Chinese eggplant, chopped into ¾-inch pieces

½ pound Thai eggplant, chopped into ¾-inch pieces

1 head cauliflower, broken into 1½-inch pieces

2 tablespoons extra-virgin olive oil

6 garlic cloves, coarsely chopped

Heaping ¼ cup coarsely chopped peeled fresh ginger

2 tablespoons soy sauce

(Not Really) Basic Rice (page 165), for serving

Chopped fresh cilantro, for serving (optional)

num pang it

Holy Trinity (page 39; use Chili-Soy Mayo), toasted baguette

1   **ROAST THE EGGPLANT:** Adjust one oven rack to the upper-middle position and one to the lower-middle position and preheat the oven to 375°F.

2   Put the tomato paste, 1 teaspoon of the salt, and ½ teaspoon of the pepper in a roasting pan or baking dish and whisk in 1¾ cups water. Add the eggplant, toss to combine, and cover the pan with aluminum foil. Set the eggplant on the upper rack and cook until it is very soft, about 1 hour.

3   **AT THE SAME TIME, ROAST THE CAULIFLOWER:** Spread the cauliflower on a rimmed baking sheet, drizzle with the oil, season with the remaining 1 teaspoon salt and ½ teaspoon pepper and toss to combine. Roast the cauliflower on the lower rack (beneath the eggplant) until it is golden brown around the edges and a fork easily slides into the center of a floret, 20 to 25 minutes.

4   Remove the eggplant from the oven, discard the foil, and let cool slightly. Transfer the slightly cooled eggplant and any liquid from the pan to a blender or food processor with the garlic, ginger, and soy sauce. Puree until smooth, then taste and adjust the flavor with more salt, pepper, and soy sauce, if needed.

5   Spoon a generous portion of eggplant onto each plate and top with some of the cauliflower. Serve with rice, sprinkled with cilantro, if desired.

salt-and-pepper yams with swiss chard

We have a few vegetarian sandwiches on our menu and the goal is always the same: to ensure that a vegetable sandwich tastes as savory and "complete" as a meaty *pang.* Yams have a very strong flavor—we roast them simply, then top them with Swiss chard notched up with lots of sautéed red onions. The chard adds an extra layer of texture and a hint of bitterness that counters the sweetness of the yam. We highly recommend adding a pickle on the side of this dish. See Put a Pickle on It (page 134) for loads of sweet-and-sour inspiration.

YAMS

4 medium yams, peeled and cut into 1-inch thick rounds

2½ tablespoons canola oil

1 teaspoon kosher salt

½ teaspoon ground black pepper

1 tablespoon sugar

SWISS CHARD

2 tablespoons canola oil

2 medium red onions, halved and thinly sliced

3 bunches Swiss chard, stemmed and leaves cut into 3-inch pieces

1 teaspoon kosher salt

1 teaspoon sugar

½ teaspoon ground black pepper

Extra-virgin olive oil, for serving

Pickles (pages 134 to 144), for serving (optional)

heads-up

In place of the Swiss chard, try spinach (it cooks in a fraction of the time), beet greens, kale, mustard greens (for a pungent and peppery taste), or collards (you may need to up the sauté time for collards).

num pang it

Holy Trinity (page 39; use Chili-Soy Mayo), toasted baguette

1   **MAKE THE YAMS:** Preheat the oven to 400°F. In a large bowl, toss the yams with the oil, salt, and pepper. Arrange the yams on a rimmed baking sheet and sprinkle the sugar over the top. Roast until lightly browned and a paring knife easily slides into the center of a yam slice, 8 to 10 minutes.

2   **MAKE THE SWISS CHARD:** Heat the canola oil in a large skillet over medium-high heat. Add the onions, reduce the heat to medium, and cook, stirring occasionally, until the onions are soft and caramelized, 8 to 10 minutes (reduce the heat to medium-low if the onions start to brown). Stir in the chard, salt, sugar, and pepper and cook, stirring occasionally, until the chard wilts, 6 to 8 minutes.

3   Divide the yams among four plates and serve with the Swiss chard, a drizzle of olive oil, and pickles.

VARIATION: LOADED SWEET POTATOES Preheat the oven to 375°F. Prick 4 sweet potatoes with the tines of a fork, then wrap each in aluminum foil and roast until a paring knife easily slides into the center of the largest potato, about 1 hour. Unwrap the potatoes and slice a slit in the center of each. Adjust an oven rack to the upper-middle position and preheat the broiler to high. Drizzle the sweet potato with a generous spoonful of honey, then season with salt and pepper. Return the potatoes to the baking sheet and broil until the top starts to caramelize, 2 to 4 minutes (watch the potatoes closely, as broiler intensities vary). Remove the potatoes from the oven, top with the Swiss chard and a drizzle of oil, and serve with the pickles, if desired.

spicy glazed tofu

———

Marinated with soy sauce, garlic, and ginger, then seared and basted in a skillet, this tofu is all about caramelized edges and a deep, nutty flavor. It develops a soft bitterness as the sugar in the soy sauce concentrates and even burns a little in the hot pan. You can serve this with just about anything—we usually opt for sautéed leeks (page 114) or Swiss chard (page 131).

1 pound extra-firm tofu, cut crosswise into ½-inch-thick pieces

1¼ cups soy sauce

1 cup honey

¼ cup sugar

2½ teaspoons finely chopped peeled fresh ginger

2½ teaspoons finely chopped fresh garlic

¾ teaspoon cayenne pepper

½ teaspoon freshly ground black pepper

½ teaspoon ground dried Thai bird's eye chile

1 teaspoon toasted sesame oil

Steamed jasmine rice, for serving

Sautéed Leeks (page 114) or Swiss Chard (page 131), for serving

heads-up

The tofu needs to chill out in the marinade for at least 6 hours in the fridge, so plan accordingly.

num pang it

Holy Trinity (page 39; use Chili-Soy Mayo), toasted baguette

1   Place the tofu in an airtight container so it all lies flat in one layer. In a medium bowl, whisk together the soy sauce, honey, sugar, ginger, garlic, cayenne, black pepper, and ground chile, then pour enough of the sauce over the tofu to cover it (cover and refrigerate the rest to use for cooking the tofu). Refrigerate the tofu for at least 6 hours or overnight.

2   Remove the tofu from the marinade. Heat a nonstick skillet over low heat. Pour about one-quarter of the reserved marinade into the pan and once it starts to sizzle, add about half the tofu, taking care not to overcrowd the pan. Pour a little marinade from the container into the skillet so the tofu is covered. Cook the tofu, occasionally spooning the marinade over the tofu, until it is nicely glazed and caramelized, 2 to 3 minutes. Carefully turn the tofu strips over and cook on other side, occasionally spooning marinade over the tofu, until it is caramelized, 2 to 3 minutes more. Repeat with the remaining marinade and tofu.

3   Serve drizzled with the sesame oil with steamed rice and sautéed leeks alongside.

PART TWO

put a pickle on it

PICKLES ARE AN enormous part of Cambodian cuisine. In fact, at every meal and on every table you will find three to five pickles served alongside mains, sides, and soups. They wake up the palate and provide a really important flavor and texture contrast to many of the hearty, fatty, and unctuous braises and meaty dishes that we like to make. The flavor palate for pickles in Cambodia is sweeter than the very tangy, acidic, and salty pickles you find in the United States, and that's the profile we use for our pickles. All the pickle recipes in this chapter are refrigerator pickles that should be eaten within a couple of weeks of making. When stored too long in the pickling liquid, ingredients like daikon, bean sprouts, and Asian pears will lose their desirable snap. For this reason, we don't recommend hot-water processing (canning) our pickles. Good thing every one of these recipes can be made quickly, with some not even requiring long pickling times (if you're an impatient pickler, check out the Pickled Bean Sprouts on page 138 and Pickled Daikon on page 139). Pickles aren't even a question for us—they're a must. We hope they become a constant on your table, too.

pickled green apples

Green mango pickle is one of the most popular pickles in Cambodia. The flavor of the green mango (which is a specific variety of mango and not just an underripe mango) is sour, while the brine is sweet—it's a really unique combination. You just can't easily find green mangoes here in the States; you can sometimes find them in Chinatown or Asian grocery stores, but to serve the pickle in the shops, we'd need them in such volume that it just wouldn't be practical. So instead, we have somewhat mimicked the flavor using Granny Smith apples. Apples are more porous than green mangoes so the texture is a bit different, but overall the effect is fairly similar.

⅓ cup plus 2 tablespoons sugar

2 tablespoons kosher salt

3 cups rice vinegar

5 Granny Smith apples, peeled, halved, cored, and sliced ¼-inch thick

1   In a medium bowl, whisk together 1 cup tepid water with the sugar and salt until both have dissolved. Pour the mixture into a resealable 2-quart container and add the vinegar and apples, making sure the apples are submerged.

2   Cover the container and refrigerate for at least 3 days before using. The pickles can be kept for up to 1 month.

KNOW THIS: EVERYTHING TASTES BETTER WITH PICKLES

Pickles taste good with everything. Don't believe us? Here's a few ideas to get you started.

- On a sandwich (um, yeah, naturally)
- Chopped and stirred into chili mayo (or plain mayo)
- Chopped and stirred into mustard
- Used to top a bowl of soup
- Added to steamed white rice
- Stirred into noodles
- Chopped and whisked into a vinaigrette

- Added to a salad
- Rolled in seaweed to make maki rolls
- Fused into a grilled cheese (or a panini)
- Added to raw slaw
- Add a little brine to your favorite green juice (really!)
- Use the brine to spike a cocktail and the pickle to garnish it

pickled bean sprouts

Bean sprouts absorb the flavor of the rice vinegar brine quickly and become lanky, acid-wielding flavor bombs. Pickled sprouts are great with intensely rich or spicy food, like the peppery halibut on page 188. For the sprouts to retain their snap and crunch, it's important to not let the bean sprouts come to a boil when they're being blanched in the water. Watch for wisps of steam rising off the top, then pull them off the heat right away.

4 cups fresh bean sprouts

2 tablespoons rice vinegar

2 tablespoons kosher salt

1½ tablespoons distilled white vinegar

1 teaspoon freshly ground black pepper

1   Fill a medium saucepan with 1 inch of water, then add the bean sprouts. Set the saucepan over medium-high heat. As soon as you notice steam rising off the top of the water, 3 to 4 minutes, remove the saucepan from the heat.

2   Add the rice vinegar, salt, white vinegar, and pepper, stir to combine, then set aside to cool to room temperature. The flavor of the sprouts will become more intense as they sit in the brine. Serve once cool (after about 1 hour), or transfer to a quart-size container, cover, and refrigerate for up to a few weeks.

pickled daikon

Daikon is a thick, cylindrical root vegetable that has a celery-like crispness with the bite and sharp flavor of a radish. When pickled, daikon keeps its crunch, while the heat and bitterness add complexity in pickle form. It's best eaten within a few days of making since the daikon loses its potency the longer it sits in the brine; but that said, it will keep in the fridge for up to a few weeks. We like this pickle with crispy quail (page 158) or braised pork belly (page 78).

1½ cups apple cider vinegar

3 tablespoons sugar

1½ teaspoons kosher salt

Heaping ⅛ teaspoon ground dried Thai bird's eye chile

1 large daikon, peeled and cut crosswise into very thin (1/16-inch-thick) rounds (a mandoline is your best bet)

In a medium bowl, whisk together the vinegar, sugar, salt, and chile until the sugar and salt have dissolved. Add the daikon and set aside for at least 20 minutes, or transfer to a quart-size container, cover, and refrigerate for up to a few weeks.

pickled asian pears

Asian pears have a subtle sweetness and a nice, snappy firmness, making them ideal for pickling. In the spring, we substitute an equal weight of rhubarb (about 1¼ pounds) for the Asian pears. The rhubarb adds a sweet-tart taste that works nicely with the pickling spices and is excellent against the richness of pork, like the Glazed Five-Spice Pork Belly (page 78) or any fatty meat.

3 Asian pears, halved, cored, and thinly sliced crosswise

3 tablespoons whole coriander seeds

3 tablespoons fennel seeds

2 tablespoons whole black peppercorns

2 dried red chiles

2 whole cloves

3¾ cups apple cider vinegar

1½ cups sugar

¾ cup finely chopped peeled fresh ginger

⅓ cup kosher salt

1   Place the Asian pears in a large heat-safe container or a quart-size mason jar.

2   In a heavy-bottomed pot, combine the coriander seeds, fennel seeds, peppercorns, chiles, and cloves. Set the pot over medium heat and toast the spices, shaking the pot often, until the spices are fragrant, about 2 minutes. Turn off the heat and add the vinegar, sugar, ginger, and salt, stirring until the sugar and salt have dissolved.

3   Ladle the hot brine over the pears and cover the container. Let cool at room temperature, and once the container is cool, refrigerate overnight before using. The pickles can be kept for up to 2 weeks.

pickled red cabbage

The texture and absorbency of thinly sliced cabbage makes it a great pickle candidate. In Cambodia, green cabbage is used predominantly, but because red cabbage is so colorful, we like to use it for pickles. Pickled cabbage is a great garnish for fried rice, noodles, and even soups (like the Curried Red Lentil Soup on page 173). It's a natural with the brisket on page 91—kind of like a Cambodian take on barbecue!

1 cup sugar

½ teaspoon kosher salt

3 cups apple cider vinegar

½ cup distilled white vinegar

1 small head red cabbage, cored and very thinly sliced (about 9 cups)

1 dried red chile

1   In a medium bowl, whisk together the sugar, salt, and ½ cup tepid water until both the sugar and salt have dissolved. Pour the mixture into a resealable container and add the apple cider vinegar, white vinegar, and cabbage, pressing down on the cabbage to submerge it. Rip the chile in half and shake the seeds into the liquid, then add the chile halves.

2   Cover the container and refrigerate for at least 3 days before using. The pickles can be kept for up to 1 month.

pickled trotters

———

Pickles are beer-drinking food for Cambodians—Americans have pretzels and peanuts, and Cambodians have pickled pig's feet and daikon! Pickled trotters will never be on the menu at Num Pang, but that said, it's a really traditional Cambodian pickle, one that is as common as a dill pickle on a hot dog. It's cartilage-y in a good way—if you like chicken feet, you've got to try trotters. Serve these with some pickled daikon and bean sprouts and you might as well be in Phnom Penh.

1¾ pounds pig trotters (about 2), halved lengthwise

3 teaspoons kosher salt

¾ cup apple cider vinegar

4 garlic cloves, smashed

1½ cups distilled white vinegar

2 fresh Thai bird's eye chiles, slit down the middle to expose the seeds (leave the ends intact)

heads-up

Save a step and ask your butcher to halve the pig trotters for you.

1   Place the trotters in a large bowl, cover with cold water, and swish around. Pour off the water and repeat. Sprinkle the trotters with 1 teaspoon of the salt and set them in a medium saucepan. Add enough water just to cover the trotters, then add ¼ cup of the apple cider vinegar and 2 of the garlic cloves. Bring the liquid to a boil over high heat, then reduce the heat to medium-low and cook the trotters very slowly, turning them occasionally, until the bones come loose and can be pulled right out of the feet, about 2 hours (add water to cover the trotters as needed). Turn off the heat and let the trotters cool completely in the liquid.

2   Once the trotters are cool, pull out and discard the bones. Place the trotters in a 2-quart container.

3   In a separate medium saucepan, combine the white vinegar, remaining ½ cup apple cider vinegar, remaining garlic, the chiles, and remaining 2 teaspoons salt. Bring the liquid to a boil over high heat, turn off the heat, and let the brine cool to room temperature. Pour the cooled brine over the trotters, cover the container, and refrigerate for 5 days before using. To serve, cut the trotters crosswise into ¼-inch-thick slices. The trotters will keep in the refrigerator for up to 1 month.

5 pickles, 1 brine

These five pickle varieties all get created, more or less, in the same brine. We switch out the type of vinegar in a couple of them, but the quantities and ratios remain identical across the board. We suggest you make a couple of pickles and always have them stashed in the fridge. They make even a plain bowl of rice into something interesting and delicious.

THE BRINE

3 cups hot water

2½ cups sugar

3 dried Thai bird's eye chiles

2 fresh rosemary sprigs

2 fresh thyme sprigs

1 tablespoon kosher salt

1 tablespoon whole black peppercorns

1 tablespoon yellow mustard seeds

½ jalapeño, quartered

6 cups rice vinegar

Vegetables (see right for quantities)

1 **MAKE THE BRINE:** In a large container or pot, combine the hot water, sugar, chiles, rosemary, thyme, salt, peppercorns, mustard seeds, and jalapeño and whisk until the sugar has dissolved. Stir in the vinegar.

2 Add the vegetables, pressing down on them to completely submerge. Cover and refrigerate for at least 24 hours or up to several weeks (some pickles stay good for 2 weeks, some for 4 weeks).

PICKLED WATERMELON RIND Peel 1 baby watermelon, halve it, then separate the white rind from the fruit. The white rind is what you save to pickle. This pickle keeps for up to a few months in the refrigerator. **Makes 1 quart.**

PICKLED LONG BEANS Cut 2 pounds long beans crosswise into thirds. Use apple cider vinegar instead of rice vinegar. This pickle keeps in the refrigerator for up to a few months. **Makes 3 quarts.**

PICKLED DAIKON AND CELERY ROOT Peel 1 medium celery root and 1 large daikon, then slice each into ⅛-inch-thick pieces (a mandoline works well). Use apple cider vinegar instead of rice vinegar. This pickle keeps in the refrigerator for up to a few months. **Makes 3 quarts.**

PICKLED KIRBIES Slice 12 Kirby cucumbers crosswise into ⅛-inch-thick rounds. Use distilled white vinegar instead of rice vinegar. This pickle keeps in the refrigerator for up to a few weeks. **Makes 3 quarts.**

SPICY PICKLED KIRBIES Slice 12 Kirby cucumbers lengthwise into ⅛-inch-thick planks. Use distilled white vinegar instead of rice vinegar and add 6 dried Thai bird's eye chiles (cut crosswise into thirds) to the brine. This pickle keeps in the refrigerator for up to a few weeks. **Makes 3 quarts.**

PART THREE

on the side

THE ASIAN TABLE is all about sharing and flooding a table with a multitude of plates, bowls, and platters of braised meats, pickles, rice dishes, noodles, soups, and condiments. Everyone sits down to eat, and bowls and plates pass from one end of the table to the other, everyone taking little bits of this and a spoonful of that, accompanied by lots of animated conversation and laughter. In short, delicious mealtime chaos! While the table scene might seem frenetic and disorderly, every eater has a very specific dinner plate goal: build a well-balanced plate. Something spicy, something cooling, something crunchy, something tender. There really isn't any one "main dish," but rather an accumulation of spoonfuls that all add up to your meal. The recipes in this chapter are all those we consider "in addition to . . ." So if you're serving pulled pork (page 73), you might also add a platter of chicken wings (page 162) to the table, some grilled corn showered with toasted coconut (page 155), and rice (page 165), of course. It's a great way to eat that keeps your palate energized and engaged.

shrimp summer rolls

Making summer rolls is a group event in many Southeast Asian homes, much like making tamales and dumplings are for Mexican and Chinese families. It's such a time-intensive process that it's more enjoyable with helping hands crowded around a kitchen island or table, with lots of storytelling and laughing, and summer roll filling and rolling of course. Summer rolls are best eaten the day they are made, so bring your appetite and a good story or two and be prepared for a memorable afternoon.

SHRIMP

1 tablespoon rice vinegar

1 tablespoon kosher salt

16 large (21/26-count) peeled and deveined shrimp

SUMMER ROLLS

4 ounces rice vermicelli noodles (see The Num Pang Pantry, page 29)

4 scallions

8 fresh mint leaves

2 Bibb lettuce leaves, torn in half (to yield 4 pieces)

8 round rice paper wrappers, for serving

About ½ cup bean sprouts (about 6 per roll)

Tuk Trey Sauce (page 168), for dipping

1 **POACH THE SHRIMP:** Fill a bowl with ice and water and set aside. Bring 4 cups water to a simmer in a medium saucepan. Add the vinegar and salt and stir until dissolved. Reduce the heat to low so you can just see steam rising off the surface of the liquid, then add the shrimp. Poach the shrimp until they curl slightly and turn opaque, 2 to 3 minutes. Transfer the shrimp to the ice bath to chill and stop the cooking, then remove the shrimp, blot them dry, and halve them lengthwise.

2 **MAKE THE SUMMER ROLLS:** Bring a medium saucepan of water to a boil. Add the rice noodles and cook following the package instructions until they are al dente, 5 to 7 minutes.

3 Trim the scallions so they are just slightly longer than the rice paper wrappers and place them in a bowl. Place the rice noodles, mint leaves, and lettuce in 3 separate bowls. Fill a medium bowl with lukewarm water, add a rice paper wrapper to the water, and moisten both sides thoroughly. Set aside (they will continue to soften as you fill them, there's no need to soak them) and repeat with the remaining wrappers.

This recipe makes enough to serve four people, but really, summer rolls are fun to make for a big group. Feel free to double or quadruple the recipe to make enough to feed a crowd.

4   Set a sheet of plastic wrap on your cutting board (this helps prevent sticking) and place a wrapper on the plastic wrap. Place 4 shrimp halves on the lower third of the wrapper. Lay the mint leaves on top of the shrimp and set 1 scallion north of the shrimp (directly on the wrapper). Add one-quarter of the noodles above the scallion and a small piece of lettuce above the noodles, along with a few bean sprouts. Fold in the ends of the summer roll like a burrito, then roll it from bottom to top in a tight bundle. Repeat with the remaining wrappers and fillings. Slice the rolls in half and serve with the sauce for dipping.

VARIATION: PORK SUMMER ROLLS Place 4 very thin slices cooked pork (such as the Orange-Glazed Spicy Pork Steak) over the shrimp, then follow the recipe as instructed.

VARIATION: HOISIN DIPPING SAUCE Mix ¼ cup hoisin sauce with 2 tablespoons Tuk Trey Sauce (page 168) and sprinkle with a spoonful of crushed roasted peanuts and half a chopped fresh Thai bird's eye chile or a drop or two of chile oil before serving with the summer rolls.

pickled fried green tomatoes

When you think fried green tomatoes, you probably think of the South—along with sweet tea and biscuits, right? But really, the acidity and brightness of green tomatoes makes them a totally suitable counterpoint to the sharp flavors of the Southeast Asian kitchen—like shrimp paste, soy sauce, and the funk of fish sauce. We use green tomatoes in a few recipes in this book, like the mussels on page 191 and the Oxtail Stew on page 183. Green tomatoes can be tough to find and expensive, too, so we often substitute large tomatillos instead (husk and rinse well before using). Here, green tomatoes get pickled before breading and frying. They're so crazy good with chili mayo on the side . . . but that said, exercise your self-control and *please* save a few for a *num pang*—you won't regret it!

PICKLED GREEN TOMATOES

1 cup distilled white vinegar

½ cup apple cider vinegar

8 garlic cloves

1 medium white onion, quartered

4 jalapeños, halved lengthwise

½ cup kosher salt

¼ cup light brown sugar

4 large green tomatoes, cut crosswise into ½-inch-thick rounds

FRIED TOMATOES

4 large eggs

3 tablespoons whole milk

2 cups panko bread crumbs

½ cup all-purpose flour

3 cups peanut oil

½ teaspoon kosher salt

¼ teaspoon cayenne pepper

¼ teaspoon sweet paprika

½ cup Most Important Chili Mayo (page 40), for serving

num pang it

Holy Trinity (page 39), toasted baguette

1   **PICKLE THE TOMATOES:** In a medium pot, combine the white vinegar, apple cider vinegar, garlic, onion, jalapeños, salt, sugar, and 4 cups water and bring to a boil while stirring occasionally. Turn off the heat and let cool to room temperature. Put the tomatoes in a large airtight container and cover with the cooled brine. Cover and refrigerate for 1 week.

2   **FRY THE TOMATOES:** Whisk the eggs and milk together in a medium bowl. Put the bread crumbs in a shallow dish and the flour in a separate shallow dish. In a large, deep skillet, heat the oil over medium-high heat until it registers 360°F on an instant-read thermometer.

3   Remove the tomatoes from the brine and pat dry. In a small bowl, mix together the salt, cayenne, and paprika. Season both sides of each tomato with the seasoned salt, then drag each tomato through the flour mixture, evenly coating both sides and patting off any excess. Dunk each tomato in the egg mixture, then coat both sides with bread crumbs. Fry the tomatoes, without overcrowding the pan, until browned on both sides, about 4 minutes. Serve with the chili mayo.

heads-up

The green tomatoes need 1 week to pickle before you can bread and fry them.

roasted okra with cauliflower crema

When we started our happy hour menu, we wanted to offer happy hour–friendly finger foods, like chicken wings (page 162) and corn on the cob (page 155). This recipe was developed to make our vegetarian friends happy. The okra roasts up super crisp, almost like potato chips, and the cauliflower dip is creamy and substantial, but the flavors—honey, sambal, pepper—are totally Num Pang.

OKRA

1 pound whole okra

1½ tablespoons canola oil

½ teaspoon kosher salt

½ teaspoon freshly ground black pepper

CAULIFLOWER CREMA

1 medium head cauliflower, cored

2 tablespoons canola oil

1¼ teaspoons kosher salt, plus more as needed

¾ teaspoon freshly ground black pepper, plus more as needed

3 to 4 tablespoons full-fat plain yogurt

2 tablespoons honey

1 tablespoon sambal oelek (see The Num Pang Pantry, page 29)

2 tablespoons finely chopped fresh cilantro leaves

1 tablespoon store-bought fried onions (see The Num Pang Pantry, page 28)

heads-up

Store-bought fried onions (see The Num Pang Pantry, page 28) are perfect over the cauliflower crema. If you can't find them, you can either caramelize onions, or use chopped scallions instead.

1   **ROAST THE OKRA:** Preheat the oven to 450°F. Place the okra on a rimmed baking sheet and toss with the oil, salt, and pepper. Roast the okra until it is crispy and browned, shaking the pan occasionally to ensure even browning, about 30 minutes.

2   **WHILE THE OKRA ROASTS, MAKE THE CAULIFLOWER CREMA:** Break the cauliflower into large florets, then thinly slice each floret. Place the cauliflower in a large bowl and toss with the oil, 1 teaspoon of the salt and ½ teaspoon of the pepper. Heat a large pot over medium heat for 1 minute, then add the cauliflower (you don't want to overcrowd the pan, so cook the cauliflower in batches if necessary). Cook gently, stirring occasionally, until the cauliflower starts to become tender (you don't want it to brown), 8 to 10 minutes. Add ½ cup water, cover the pot, and steam the cauliflower until it is fork-tender, about 10 minutes. Drain the cauliflower if needed and set aside to cool.

3   Transfer half the cooled cauliflower to a food processor and add 2 tablespoons of the yogurt, 1 tablespoon of the honey and 1½ teaspoons of the sambal. Process until smooth, then scrape the mixture into a medium bowl. Repeat with the remaining cauliflower, yogurt, honey, sambal, salt, and pepper. Once smooth, stir this mixture into the first batch, taste, and add more salt or pepper if needed.

4   Sprinkle the cauliflower crema with the cilantro and fried onions. Serve alongside the roasted okra.

roasted winter vegetables

We have two Num Pang locations within a stone's throw of the greenmarket in New York City's Union Square and have come to use it as a constant source of seasonal inspiration. For our roasted vegetable side dish, we switch up the vegetables throughout the year to highlight whatever is plentiful and available. Drizzled with our Garlic Chive Vinaigrette (page 213), this is a side dish that, with a side of steamed rice or a nicely cooked piece of protein, could easily be the main component of a healthy meal.

3 cups medium Brussels sprouts, halved

3 large carrots, halved crosswise, then quartered lengthwise

3 tablespoons extra-virgin olive oil

1 tablespoon plus 2 teaspoons kosher salt

1 teaspoon freshly ground black pepper

1 lemongrass stalk, tough outer layer removed, tender inner core finely chopped (about 1 tablespoon)

1 pound long beans or green beans, cut into 5-inch lengths (if using green beans, halve them crosswise on an angle)

2 medium red onions, cut into ½-inch-thick rounds

Garlic Chive Vinaigrette (page 213)

1   Preheat the oven to 400°F. Place the Brussels sprouts on one rimmed baking sheet and the carrot quarters on a second rimmed baking sheet. Season each batch of vegetables with 1 tablespoon of the oil, ½ teaspoon of the salt, and ¼ teaspoon of the pepper; add the lemongrass to the carrots. Roast the Brussels sprouts until the outsides are caramelized and the tip of a paring knife easily slides into the center of a sprout, about 30 minutes. Roast the carrots until tender and caramelized around the edges, about 40 minutes total. As they finish roasting, transfer the sprouts and carrots to a large bowl.

2   Fill a large bowl with ice and water and set aside. Bring a large saucepan of water to a boil and add 1 tablespoon of the salt and the long beans (or green beans). Blanch the beans until they are tender, 2 to 5 minutes (green beans will cook faster than long beans). Use a slotted spoon to transfer the beans to the ice water bath to stop the cooking, then transfer them to a paper towel–lined plate to drain briefly. Add the beans to the bowl with the sprouts and carrots.

3   Heat a charcoal or gas grill to medium-high, or heat a grill pan over medium-high heat. Brush both sides of each onion slice with the remaining 1 tablespoon olive oil, then season with the remaining 1 teaspoon salt and ½ teaspoon pepper. Grill the onions on both sides until grill marked and starting to soften and caramelize, 8 to 10 minutes.

4   Add the onions to the bowl with the other vegetables. Drizzle with some of the vinaigrette and toss to combine. Serve warm.

VARIATION: ROASTED SPRING VEGETABLES If you can find spring onions, substitute them for the red onions (spring onions tend to be smaller than red onions, so use 4). Instead of Brussels sprouts, snap off the tough ends from 1 pound asparagus, brush with olive oil, season with salt and pepper, and grill in a grill pan or on a charcoal or gas grill until tender. Roast the carrots, cook the long beans (or green beans), and dress the vegetables as instructed.

VARIATION: ROASTED SUMMER VEGETABLES Substitute Vidalia onions for the red onions. Instead of Brussels sprouts, quarter 2 zucchini and 2 yellow squash lengthwise, brush with olive oil, season with salt and pepper, and grill in a grill pan or on a charcoal or gas grill until tender. Roast the carrots (halve the amounts of oil, salt, and pepper), cook the long beans (or green beans), and dress the vegetables as instructed.

chili-coconut grilled corn

You can't live in New York City during the summertime without getting at least one fix of Mexican grilled corn on a stick. Slathered with mayonnaise and crema, doused with fresh lime juice, and finished with a few pinches of chili powder and cilantro, the corn hits just about every sweet-sour-bitter-spicy-acidic point. At Num Pang, we finish parboiled corn on the grill with melted butter, then top it off with a squeeze of Most Important Chili Mayo (page 40), coconut flakes, chili powder, and lime. Our favorite corn is the bicolor variety that has both white and yellow kernels—it's sweet and rich in all the right ways. You can also ax the blanching step and grill the corn in the husks (soak the ears for 20 minutes prior to grilling over a medium-low flame), or for a more flame-kissed taste, grill the ears without the husk straight over the fire for about 10 minutes.

2 tablespoons kosher salt, plus more as needed

4 ears corn, husked

4 tablespoons (2 ounces) unsalted butter, melted

Most Important Chili Mayo, Chili-Soy Mayo, or Chili Yogurt (page 40)

¼ cup untoasted unsweetened desiccated coconut

Chili powder (the kind you use for making chili)

1 lime, cut into wedges

1   Bring a large pot of water to a boil over high heat. Add the salt and the corn. Once the water returns to a boil, cover the pot and cook the corn for 1½ minutes. Transfer the corn to a paper towel–lined plate to drain.

2   Heat a charcoal or gas grill to medium-high. Brush the corn with the melted butter and set it on the grill, cooking the corn on all sides until the kernels caramelize and frequently brushing the corn with more butter, 2 to 3 minutes. Transfer the corn to a platter and sprinkle with salt.

3   Liberally coat each grilled ear of corn with chili mayo. Sprinkle with some of the coconut, then a pinch of chili powder. Serve each ear with a lime wedge.

heads-up

Skip shredded sweetened flaked coconut in the baking aisle of your supermarket. For a true and honest coconut flavor, look for fine particles of desiccated coconut that is untoasted and unsweetened (see The Num Pang Pantry, page 36, for more info).

fried smelt with matcha-chile salt

Smelt, whiting, and baitfish: these small fish are fantastic fried and eaten head, bones, and all. Call a few fishmongers ahead of time and try to find the smallest ones you can—about 1 inch in length is ideal. If you can't find tiny little guys and have to buy bigger ones, just ask your fishmonger to chop of the heads and bone 'em out for you. Here we serve them piled up on a platter, with a seasoned coarse salt made with matcha, a very vibrant kind of powdered green tea, and cayenne pepper. These are fantastic eaten like popcorn while you're hanging out watching TV . . . or pile them onto a baguette for a killer *num pang*.

MATCHA-CHILE SALT

2 tablespoons matcha green tea powder

1½ tablespoons kosher salt

¾ teaspoon cayenne pepper

SMELT

2 cups peanut oil

1 pound smelt, whiting, or baitfish (preferably 1 inch long—if they are longer than 1 inch, split and remove the bones)

½ teaspoon kosher salt

¼ teaspoon freshly ground black pepper

1 cup all-purpose flour

3 tablespoons cornstarch

1 lime, cut into wedges, for serving

Pickled Daikon (page 139), for serving

num pang it

Holy Trinity (page 39), toasted baguette

1   **MAKE THE MATCHA-CHILE SALT:** In a small bowl, mix together the matcha tea powder, salt, and cayenne until well combined.

2   **MAKE THE SMELT:** In a medium skillet, heat the oil over medium-high heat until it registers 350°F to 360°F on an instant-read thermometer. While the oil heats, season the smelt with the salt and pepper and set aside. In a large bowl, whisk the flour, cornstarch, and 1 cup cold water together until smooth.

3   Dip the smelt in the batter one by one, letting the excess batter drip off before adding them to the hot oil. Fry the smelt, using a chopstick or slotted spoon to keep them from sticking together and turning them often, until they are golden brown on both sides, 2 to 3 minutes total. Use a spider to transfer the fried smelt to a paper towel–lined plate to drain. Squeeze the lime wedges over the smelt and dip into the matcha-chile salt. Serve with the pickled daikon on the side.

crispy fried quail with thai chiles

There's not a whole lot of meat on a little quail, which is why we think of this dish as a side dish rather than a main course. The key to cooking quail to a perfect, shatteringly crisp, sticky-sweet state is to slowly render the fat out of the skin in a skillet, then drizzle it with maple syrup and blast it in a hot oven to finish cooking. As with all our food, we like to balance the crispy-sweetness of the quail with something pickled, in this case daikon (page 139), and something salty and spicy like the fresh bird's eye chile salt. In Cambodia, you'd get this with some Tuk Trey Sauce (page 168) on the side for dipping. If you can't find quail, you can absolutely substitute Cornish hens.

2 tablespoons plus 1¾ teaspoons kosher salt

½ teaspoon freshly ground black pepper

4 quails, rib bones removed

2 tablespoons chicken fat, bacon fat, or grapeseed oil

2 fresh Thai bird's eye chiles or red serranos, very finely chopped

4 teaspoons maple syrup

2 scallions, thinly sliced on an angle

Coarsely chopped fresh cilantro, for serving

Pickled Daikon (page 139), for serving (optional)

Chile Salt (page 50), for serving (optional)

1   Preheat the oven to 350°F. Mix 1½ teaspoons of the salt and the pepper in a small bowl, then use it to season both sides of each quail. Heat a large oven-safe skillet over medium-high heat and add the chicken fat. Swirl the fat around in the pan and pour out the excess (you can save it to use another time). Set the quail in the pan, back-side down, reduce the heat to medium, and cook until the quail is nicely browned, 5 to 6 minutes. Turn the quail over and brown the other side, 5 to 6 minutes more.

2   While the quail browns, make the chile salt: Use a mortar and pestle to pulverize 2 tablespoons of the salt with the chiles until the mixture is wet and the chiles are totally smashed into the salt. Set aside.

3   Transfer the skillet with the quail to the oven and cook until the juices at the leg joint run clean, about 5 minutes (or 8 minutes, if using Cornish hens). Remove the quail from the oven and drizzle 1 teaspoon of the maple syrup over each quail. Turn each quail over and sprinkle with the remaining ¼ teaspoon salt. Return the quail to the oven and cook until the maple syrup starts bubbling, about 1 minute more.

4   Serve the quail sprinkled with scallions and cilantro, with pickled daikon (if using), and with a small bowl of chile salt on the side for sprinkling or dipping.

tamarind baby back ribs
with cilantro-lime dipping sauce

These ribs were a must-order at Ratha's first restaurant in New York City, Kampuchea. The sauce is like a souped-up Southeast Asian version of barbecue, with tamarind pulp contributing a key sweet-sourness. Tamarind is naturally tangy, and that intensity against the porky intensity of the ribs is a total match. The ribs get braised super slow in a barely warm oven until the meat is so tender, it falls off the bone if you give it a stern look. You could eat these as your main meal, but they're really so rich and intense that we prefer them as an indulgent starter or complement to another protein, like chicken or shrimp.

RIBS

1 cup apple cider vinegar

2 tablespoons fish sauce

1½ tablespoons sugar

1 tablespoon kosher salt

1 tablespoon freshly ground
    black pepper

1½ teaspoons cayenne pepper

2 racks baby back ribs (8 ribs each)

4 lemongrass stalks, tough outer husk
    removed and discarded, tender
    inner reed finely chopped

TAMARIND SAUCE

½ block tamarind pulp (about 8 ounces;
    see The Num Pang Pantry, page 35)

2 tablespoons finely chopped
    yellow onion

½ cup sugar

3 tablespoons fish sauce

½ teaspoon fermented shrimp paste
    (see The Num Pang Pantry, page 25)

1 tablespoon kosher salt

ingredients continue

1   **MAKE THE RIBS:** Preheat the oven to 275°F.

2   In a medium bowl, whisk together the vinegar, fish sauce, sugar, salt, black pepper, cayenne, and 1 cup water. Place the ribs in a roasting pan and pour enough of the marinade in to reach halfway up each rack. Sprinkle the lemongrass over the ribs and cover the roasting pan with a sheet of aluminum foil. Prick a few vent holes in the foil using a fork. Cook the ribs until a paring knife slips into the meat meeting absolutely no resistance, 1½ to 2 hours.

3   **WHILE THE RIBS COOK, MAKE THE TAMARIND GLAZE:** In a medium saucepan, combine the tamarind pulp and 1½ cups warm water and use your fingers to pull the pulp apart into small pieces. Add the onion and bring the liquid to a boil over medium-high heat. Simmer until the tamarind starts to break down, about 10 minutes. Reduce the heat to medium-low and continue to gently simmer until it looks like a thick barbecue sauce, about 15 minutes (if it looks too thick, add a little water; if it looks too thin, continue to simmer for a few more minutes). Carefully transfer the sauce to a blender and puree until smooth. Add the sugar, fish sauce, shrimp paste, and salt and blend until smooth.

recipe continues

CILANTRO-LIME DIPPING SAUCE

1 cup finely chopped fresh cilantro

¼ cup fresh lime juice (from 3 to 4 limes)

2 teaspoons kosher salt

¼ teaspoon freshly ground black pepper

1 cup canola oil

3 scallions, finely chopped, for serving

Pickled Bean Sprouts (page 138; optional), for serving

4 **MAKE THE CILANTRO-LIME DIPPING SAUCE:** Rinse out and dry the blender, then add the cilantro, lime juice, salt, and pepper. Blend on medium speed until well combined. With the blender running, slowly add the oil a few drops at a time until the sauce is well emulsified (it should be the consistency of a very thin mayonnaise).

5 Adjust an oven rack to the top position and heat the broiler to high. Transfer the ribs to a rimmed baking sheet and divide the tamarind glaze over each rack, using a silicone brush to evenly coat both sides. Set the ribs under the broiler until they start to sizzle and the glaze begins to char, 1 to 2 minutes. Remove from the oven and slice into individual ribs. Sprinkle with scallions and serve with the pickled bean sprouts, if desired, and the cilantro-lime dipping sauce.

KNOW THIS: THE 4-1-1 ON PORK RIBS

If you have a whole pork rib roast and you separate the bones from the cylinder of meat, what you're left with is a rack of bones called baby back ribs and a boneless pork loin roast. The ribs on a pig are actually quite long and run down the entire side of the pig—the upper portion near the spine of the pig is where the pork rib roast is (and the baby back ribs). Baby back ribs are small compared to the bigger, meatier ribs from lower down toward the pig's belly. The upper rib section is also leaner and has a tendency to be more tender, with a nice, arched bone. Farther down the rib you have straight and long St. Louis–style ribs and then toward the belly is the spare rib, both of which are fattier than the baby backs.

Some meat departments will offer baby back ribs, but many don't because they are more likely to sell the ribs still attached to the pork loin and butchered into individual pork rib chops. If you can't find baby back ribs, you can totally make this recipe using the St. Louis–style rack or spareribs; just note that you'll probably have to braise the ribs for up to 1 hour longer than the recipe indicates. You know the meat is done when a paring knife easily slips into the meat meeting no resistance. Be prepared for a fattier rib, too.

sambal-glazed chicken wings

Chicken wings are huge in Cambodia where they are seasoned with salt and sugar, panfried, and then served with a thin dressing-type dip, similar to the Tuk Trey Sauce (page 168). The fried, saucy, boldly spiced chicken wings we eat in the States are a totally different beast than Cambodian wings. Here we bridge the two worlds by roasting vinegar-marinated wings and then brushing them with a sweet-spicy glaze before they take a trip under the broiler to singe and caramelize.

WINGS

¼ cup apple cider vinegar

¼ cup fish sauce

2 tablespoons soy sauce

2 tablespoons sambal oelek (see The Num Pang Pantry, page 29)

1 tablespoon kosher salt

2 teaspoons honey

¼ medium yellow onion, chopped

6 garlic cloves, smashed

2½ pounds chicken wings

GLAZE

1 cup apple cider

¾ cup orange juice

⅓ cup sambal oelek

¼ cup apple cider vinegar

¼ cup honey

¼ cup soy sauce

¼ red apple

¼ medium yellow onion, chopped

2 garlic cloves, peeled

¼ teaspoon ground dried Thai bird's eye chile

4 scallions, thinly sliced on an angle, for serving (optional)

heads-up

The wings need to marinate for 6 hours and up to overnight before roasting—which is perfect timing, since the glaze needs to simmer on the stovetop for an hour before it's ready.

1 **MARINATE THE WINGS:** In a large bowl, whisk together the vinegar, fish sauce, soy sauce, sambal, salt, and honey, until the salt has dissolved. Stir in the onion and garlic, then add the wings and toss to thoroughly coat with the marinade. Cover with bowl with plastic wrap and refrigerate for at least 6 hours or overnight.

2 **MAKE THE GLAZE:** In a large, heavy-bottomed pot, combine the apple cider, orange juice, sambal, vinegar, honey, soy sauce, apple, onion, garlic, chile, and ¾ cup water. Bring the mixture to a boil over high heat, reduce the heat to medium-low, and gently simmer (only a bubble or two should burst at the surface), stirring often, until the apple falls apart and the glaze becomes very thick and red, about 1 hour. Set aside to cool slightly, then blend until smooth (in batches, if necessary).

3 Adjust one oven rack to the upper-middle position and another to the middle position and preheat the oven to 350°F. Line a rimmed baking sheet with aluminum foil.

4 Remove the wings from the marinade, shake off any excess (a little marinade left clinging to the wings is fine), and place on the lined baking sheet. Roast on the middle rack until golden, about 25 minutes, turning the wings over about midway through cooking.

5 Transfer the wings to a large bowl and toss with the glaze. Set the broiler on high. Return the wings to the baking sheet and broil until the wings and the glaze are sizzling, 2 to 3 minutes. Serve sprinkled with the scallions, if desired.

(not really) basic rice

This is our "basic" version of rice—which executes the same flavor balance principles as our sandwiches: the rice takes the place of the bread, acting as the neutral party that benefits from the freshness of the herbs, crunch and sweetness from the fried onion and garlic, the tanginess of the lime juice, and heat from black pepper. Steam the rice, then cool it and toss it with all these bold ingredients to create a really delicious foundation for rice bowls. On its own or as an accompaniment to short ribs, braised pork, coconut shrimp, or anything, really . . . this basic rice is honestly anything but.

2 cups jasmine rice

2 tablespoons plus 1½ teaspoons kosher salt, plus more as needed

1 cup finely chopped fresh cilantro leaves

1 cup finely chopped fresh Thai or Italian basil leaves

1 cup fried onions or shallots (see The Num Pang Pantry, page 28, or page 185)

¾ cup fresh lime juice (from 7 to 8 limes), plus more as needed

½ cup fried garlic (see The Num Pang Pantry, page 28)

2¼ teaspoons freshly ground black pepper, plus more as needed

1 teaspoon canola oil

heads-up

For brown rice, increase the cooking time by 20 to 30 minutes.

1   Place the rice in a colander, set the colander in a large bowl, and cover the rice with cold water. Swish the rice around until the water gets cloudy. Lift the colander up out of the bowl and pour out the cloudy water. Repeat this process, swishing and draining the water each time, until the water is completely clear.

2   Transfer the rice to a medium saucepan and add cold water to cover by ¾ inch. Stir 2 tablespoons of the salt into the rice, cover the saucepan, and bring the liquid to a boil. Reduce the heat to medium-low, set the cover askew, and cook the rice until it has absorbed all the water, about 20 minutes. Fluff the rice with a fork, then cover the saucepan completely and let stand for 10 minutes.

3   Turn out the rice onto a rimmed baking sheet and set it aside to cool to room temperature, 15 to 20 minutes.

4   Transfer the cooled rice out to a large bowl and add the cilantro, basil, fried onion, lime juice, fried garlic, pepper, oil, and remaining 1½ teaspoons salt. Stir to combine, taste, and adjust the lime juice, salt, and pepper, if needed.

bacon fried rice

Fried rice is a beautiful thing: for breakfast with a sunny-side up egg, for lunch, or for dinner alongside coconut shrimp (page 117) or a skirt steak (page 99). The best thing about it is that it is such a great use for day-old leftover rice—which is actually the best rice to use. Cold rice holds its texture nicely and isn't too absorbent, so the rice stays fluffy and has a good bite. For a vegan version, omit the bacon and use three tablespoons of canola oil to fry the garlic; a few shakes of toasted sesame oil over the finished rice will add a subtle smoky note that goes a long way in the umami department.

6 bacon slices

8 medium garlic cloves, very thinly sliced

6 cups cooked long-grain white rice (preferably jasmine; page 29)

1½ tablespoons kosher salt

1½ tablespoons freshly ground black pepper

Juice of ¾ lime

3 scallions, thinly sliced on an angle

½ cup finely chopped fresh Thai basil leaves

1. Heat a large skillet over medium heat. Add the bacon and cook it on both sides until the fat has rendered and the bacon is crisp, 6 to 8 minutes (depending on the thickness of the bacon). Transfer the bacon to a paper towel–lined plate to drain excess fat.

2. Reduce the heat to medium-low and add the garlic to the pan. Cook, stirring often, until the garlic is fragrant and golden (don't let it brown), 30 seconds to 1 minute. Stir in the rice, salt, and pepper and cook, stirring often, until the rice is warmed through. Turn off the heat and stir in the lime juice, scallions, and basil. Crumble the bacon over the rice and stir it once or twice before serving.

green tomato hot sauce

This hot sauce takes minutes to make in a blender of food processor and goes with just about anything. As you can guess by now, we are big lovers of acidity in food, whether it comes from vinegar, a pickle, or a heat-packing hot sauce. You can make this sauce with green tomatoes when they are in season (generally early summer through the fall) or with tomatillos.

1½ pounds green tomatoes or tomatillos

1½ cups fresh cilantro leaves

2 medium fresh Thai bird's eye chiles, coarsely chopped

1 medium garlic clove, coarsely chopped

½ medium yellow onion, coarsely chopped

Juice of ½ lime, plus more as needed

½ teaspoon kosher salt, plus more as needed

1   If using green tomatoes, core them and coarsely chop. If using tomatillos, husk them, rinse away any stickiness from the surface of the tomatillos under warm water, dry them, then coarsely chop.

2   Transfer the tomatoes or tomatillos to a blender and add the cilantro, chiles, garlic, onion, lime juice, and salt. Blend until well combined. Taste and adjust with more lime juice or salt, if needed. Store in an airtight container in the refrigerator for up to 2 weeks.

tuk trey sauce

We call this our "house dressing" because it's the default vinaigrette-style sauce that we serve with our salads. Really, though, *tuk trey* sauce can be two things: it can refer to a simple fish sauce, or a more complex multi-ingredient sauce, which is what the recipe below represents. Think of it like a Cambodian version of Vietnamese *nuoc cham* sauce. It's salty, tangy, spicy, and sweet, hitting lots of flavor angles at once. We can't imagine life without it.

3 cups fish sauce

1 cup rice vinegar

½ cup cane sugar or light brown sugar

2 carrots, cut into 2-inch segments

1 large white onion, quartered

6 garlic cloves, coarsely chopped

1 (1½-inch) piece fresh ginger, peeled and smashed

3 tablespoons kosher salt

1 teaspoon hoisin sauce

1 teaspoon toasted sesame oil

1   In a medium saucepan, combine the fish sauce, vinegar, sugar, carrots, onion, garlic, ginger, salt, hoisin, and 3 cups water. Bring to a boil over high heat, stirring occasionally to dissolve the sugar and salt, then reduce the heat to medium-low and gently simmer until slightly syrupy, about 45 minutes.

2   Turn off the heat and let cool completely, then strain the sauce through a fine-mesh sieve into an airtight container. Whisk in the sesame oil and refrigerate for up to 1 month (shake well before serving).

PART FOUR

in a bowl:
hot

NOTHING QUITE SAYS COMFORT like a bowl of something warm and hearty. The soups, stews, and meals-in-a-bowl in this chapter all maintain our mantra of big, bold flavors in every spoonful. We are big into finishes and garnishes, even on soups, so don't be surprised to see Pickled Red Cabbage (page 142) appear on top of beef stew (page 184) or caramelized spiced cashews on top of Loaded Oatmeal (page 195). Flavors, textures, and contrasts—it's the Num Pang way.

curried red lentil soup

This vegan soup is really more Indian than Cambodian. Once you scan the recipe and the ingredient list (you always read the recipe before starting to cook, right?) you may think we forgot a key ingredient—the curry! Just relax—we don't add curry powder to this soup because the spices we use, like coriander, cumin, fennel, pepper, and fresh ginger, combined with the warm, fiery glow of the soup gives it a curry feel. The soup is homey and comforting on its own, but what makes it Num Pang worthy are the toppings you add at the end—the pickled carrots, pickled cabbage, fried onions, and cilantro. Fresh, pickled, crunchy, herby, tangy . . . it's like a *num pang* in a bowl.

2 tablespoons canola oil

2 tablespoons ground coriander (preferably freshly ground; see page 122)

2 tablespoons ground cumin

2 tablespoons ground fennel seed

2 tablespoons kosher salt, plus more as needed

1½ tablespoons freshly ground black pepper, plus more as needed

¼ cup finely chopped peeled fresh ginger

5 garlic cloves, finely chopped

2 medium yellow onions, finely chopped

2 medium carrots, finely chopped

1 jalapeño, finely chopped

1 pound red lentils, rinsed

1 (14-ounce) can whole tomatoes

½ bunch fresh cilantro, finely chopped

Holy Pickled Carrots (page 42)

Pickled Red Cabbage (page 142)

Store-bought fried onions (see The Num Pang Pantry, page 28)

1. In a large soup pot, heat the oil over medium heat. Add the coriander, cumin, fennel, 1 tablespoon of the salt, and the pepper and cook, stirring often, until fragrant, about 1 minute.

2. Stir in the ginger and garlic cook until fragrant, about 1 minute, then add the chopped onions, carrots, and jalapeño and cook, stirring often, until the onions are golden brown, 4 to 5 minutes.

3. Stir in the remaining salt and the lentils, then add the tomatoes and 8 cups water. Increase the heat to medium-high and bring the soup to a simmer, then reduce the heat to medium-low and simmer gently, stirring every 5 to 10 minutes to ensure nothing sticks to the bottom of the pot. Cook until the liquid has reduced by half and the lentils turn yellow in color and break down to a creamy consistency, about 45 minutes (add more water to thin the soup if needed).

4. Turn off the heat, taste, and adjust the seasoning with salt and pepper, if needed. In batches, carefully transfer the soup to a blender and puree, then return it to a clean pot and reheat if necessary (or use an immersion blender to puree the soup right in the pot). Serve garnished with the cilantro, pickled carrots, pickled cabbage, and fried onions.

ben's great-grandma's matzo ball soup

So, we realize this recipe has nothing to do with Num Pang. There isn't even *cilantro* in the soup. But we live in New York City, where matzo ball soup is as treasured as hot dogs and, well, *num pang*. Plus, we both love matzo ball soup (and regularly hit the 2nd Ave Deli for a bowl). Ben grew up on this one in particular, so we wanted to share it with you. You got a problem with that? (Hope not.) Ben's recipe came from his great-grandmother Clara, who passed it down to his grandmother Cheri, who passed it down to Mimi, Ben's mom. Now it's in your hands, so treat it kindly. For instance: it's key to make matzo balls with schmaltz—that's chicken fat to anyone outside of the fold. If you don't have a bag of scraps and excess fat in your freezer from trimming chicken pieces and breaking down whole chickens (it's a good practice to do this), then ask your butcher if he or she has chicken fat and skin tucked away behind the counter.

MATZO BALLS

1 cup chicken skin and fat

½ medium yellow onion, cut crosswise into ½-inch-thick rings

2 large eggs

½ cup matzo meal (not matzo ball mix)

2 teaspoons kosher salt

1 teaspoon freshly ground white pepper

CHICKEN SOUP

1 (3½- to 4-pound) whole chicken, cut into serving pieces

1 parsley root (if you cannot find parsley root, do not substitute parsnip; just omit the parsley root)

1 medium yellow onion, halved

2 teaspoons kosher salt

1 teaspoon finely ground white pepper

3 medium carrots, cut on an angle into ½-inch-thick pieces

3 celery stalks, cut on an angle into ½-inch-thick pieces

6 fresh dill sprigs (fronds and stems), coarsely chopped

1   **RENDER THE SCHMALTZ FOR THE THE MATZO BALLS:** In a medium heavy-bottomed skillet, cook the chicken skin and fat very gently over medium-low heat until the fat starts to render and separate out, about 10 minutes. Add the onion rings and continue to cook, stirring occasionally, until the fat has completely rendered from the skin, about 30 minutes (reduce the heat if the onions start browning—you don't want them to color). Discard the onion, set the skin on a paper towel to drain (then sprinkle with salt and eat while it's hot—cook's snack), and transfer the fat to a small heat-safe bowl to cool to room temperature (you should have ¼ cup of fat).

2   Whisk the eggs in a large bowl until they are frothy, then add the cooled chicken fat, matzo meal, salt, and pepper and use a fork to mix until well combined. Place a sheet of plastic wrap directly against the surface of the mixture and refrigerate for 2 hours or up to 2 days.

3   **MAKE THE CHICKEN SOUP:** Put the chicken in a large pot and add water to cover by 3 inches. Add the parsley root (if using) and onion, and bring the water up to a gentle simmer over medium heat. Once the water is simmering, reduce the heat to low.

When the broth is gently simmering, make sure the pot is half off the burner. The offset distribution of heat naturally pushes the froth and impurities to one side of the pot, making it easy to skim them off.

Slide the pot so it is half off the burner and skim off the foamy impurities as they rise to the surface. Cook gently for 1 hour (it should be hot enough to threaten to bubble, but not be simmering in a violent way).

4   Strain the broth through a fine-mesh sieve into a clean pot. Set the chicken breasts aside and once they are cool enough to handle, discard the skin and remove the meat from the bones. Chop the meat into bite-size pieces. Discard the wings and backbone and save the thigh and drumstick meat to use for chicken salad. Add the salt and white pepper to the broth, taste, and add more if needed. Return the broth to a simmer over medium heat. Add the carrots and celery and cook until they are just tender, even al dente (not mushy!). Remove from the heat.

5   **MAKE THE MATZO BALLS:** Remove the matzo mixture from the fridge and roll it into marble-size balls, setting them aside on a large plate as you go (work quickly—the heat from your hands will soften the mixture). Refrigerate the balls until you're ready to cook them.

6   Bring a large pot of water (a wide pot is best—surface area is more important than depth) to a boil and add 2 tablespoons salt. Reduce the heat to medium (you just want to see steam rising from the surface), add the matzo balls, and cover the pot. Simmer the matzo balls until they are cooked through and pale yellow from edge to core, about 30 minutes. Transfer the cooked matzo balls to a baking dish or container.

7   Add the chopped chicken, dill, and cooked matzo balls to the soup and cook over medium heat just until the matzo balls are warmed through, 5 to 8 minutes. Turn off the heat and serve.

butternut squash soup with coconut cream

———

Our trick to giving Num Pang's vegan butternut squash soup its deep sweet-savory taste—without relying on chicken broth—is to puree a small wedge of roasted green cabbage right into the soup. The cabbage rounds out the sweetness of the squash, apple cider, and coconut milk, adding backbone and underlying robustness.

1 (3-pound) butternut squash, peeled, halved, seeded, and chopped into 1-inch cubes

¼ pound green cabbage, halved (about one-eighth of a 2-pound head)

2 tablespoons canola oil

2½ teaspoons kosher salt

4 cups apple cider

1¼ cups coconut milk

Pinch of red pepper flakes

KNOW THIS: A MILKY COCONUT MILK

Different brands of coconut milk can have dramatically different consistencies—from thin and milky to thick and creamy—even though they are all labeled "coconut milk." If in doubt, give the can a quick shake before you buy it. You should hear an ample amount of liquid sloshing around inside. If you don't, this means that there are a lot of coconut solids in the can, which will yield a thick soup. Not the end of the world, but you will probably need to thin the soup with water (or chicken broth), and that will dilute the intensity of the soup's flavor.

1   Preheat the oven to 400°F. Combine the squash and cabbage in a large bowl and toss with the oil and 1½ teaspoons of the salt. Turn the mixture out onto a rimmed baking sheet and roast until the squash and cabbage are tender, stirring halfway through, 40 to 50 minutes (if the cabbage starts to look dark around the 30-minute mark, remove it from the baking sheet and continue to roast the squash).

2   Transfer the squash and cabbage to a blender. Add the apple cider, 1 cup of the coconut milk, the remaining 1 teaspoon salt, and the red pepper flakes. Puree until the soup is totally smooth.

3   Transfer the soup to a medium saucepan and warm it over medium-low heat, stirring often. If the soup is too thick, add water, ¼ cup at a time, until the soup reaches your preferred consistency; taste and adjust the seasoning with salt and pepper as needed.

4   Divide the soup among individual bowls. Serve drizzled with a spoonful of the remaining coconut milk.

pork bone and stuffed bitter melon soup

———

Bitter melon is a bumpy and, well, yes, very bitter vegetable (it is somewhat of an acquired taste) that has more in common with a zucchini than a honeydew. This is a very traditional soup that offers up a bowl of soulful pork bone broth with a poached ground pork–stuffed bitter melon. It's delicious and unusual, and just the thing to serve to friends who think they have seen it all.

PORK BONE STOCK

2 lemongrass stalks

4 pounds pork bones

4 large garlic cloves, lightly crushed

1 teaspoon fish sauce

1 teaspoon sugar

1 teaspoon kosher salt

BITTER MELON SOUP

2 medium bitter melons, halved crosswise

¾ pound ground pork

1 cup finely chopped scallions (white and green parts; about 16 scallions)

1 teaspoon fish sauce, plus more as needed

1 teaspoon sugar, plus more as needed

1 teaspoon kosher salt, plus more as needed

1 teaspoon freshly ground black pepper, plus more as needed

Steamed jasmine rice, for serving

1 **MAKE THE PORK BONE STOCK:** Peel back the tough outer husks of the lemongrass stalks, leaving it attached on the bottom, and wrap the tough skin around the base of the lemongrass stalk and knot it (you may have to fold the lemongrass to fit it in the pot). Put the lemongrass in a large pot with the pork bones and garlic and add water to cover by 2 inches. Bring to a boil, reduce the heat to medium-low, and simmer gently, partially covered, skimming off impurities as they rise to the surface, for 2½ hours. Turn off the heat and add the fish sauce, sugar, and salt and set aside to cool. Strain through a fine-mesh sieve set over a large bowl (discard the solids). (You should have 5 to 6 cups stock.)

2 **MAKE THE BITTER MELON SOUP:** Use a teaspoon to scoop out the seeds from the melons, so you have 4 tunneled-out halves. Mix together the pork, half of the scallions, the fish sauce, sugar, salt, and pepper. Stuff each bitter melon half with the pork mixture, packing the meat mixture in tightly, so it is compact.

3 Bring the pork stock to a simmer in a medium saucepan or Dutch oven over medium-high heat. Reduce the heat to medium-low, add the stuffed melons, and partially cover with a lid; poach until they are tender, about 20 minutes. Taste the broth—it will be very delicate. Adjust with more fish sauce, sugar, salt, or pepper.

4 Transfer the stuffed melons to a cutting board and slice each crosswise into ½-inch-thick pieces. Divide the broth among individual bowls and add a few pieces of stuffed bitter melon to each. Serve sprinkled with the remaining scallions and alongside rice.

ginger chicken in broth

Think of this as the Asian version of the classic French dish *poule au pot*, "chicken in the pot." Here, we take a small chicken, like a poussin or Cornish game hen, and gently poach it in a gingery chicken broth with aromatics like garlic and more ginger. Chayote squash and some cooked brown rice go in at the end for a truly all-in-one meal. Serve the broth in a cup on the side of chicken, which should be plated knife-and-fork style. It's a very healing, nourishing meal.

CHICKEN BROTH

1 (4-pound) chicken

1 medium yellow onion, quartered

2 garlic cloves

1 (1-inch) piece fresh ginger

CHICKEN IN THE POT

1 Cornish game hen or poussin
    (less than 3 pounds)

1 small chayote squash, chopped into
    ¾-inch pieces

⅓ cup cooked brown rice

2 garlic cloves

1 (1-inch) piece fresh ginger, peeled
    and thinly sliced on an angle

2 teaspoons kosher salt

2 teaspoons freshly ground
    black pepper

½ lime

2 scallions, thinly sliced on an angle

Chopped fresh cilantro, for serving

heads-up

Using a great homemade chicken broth is a *must*. Ours is simple but elegant; freeze leftover broth for giving any soup a soft Southeast Asian flavor.

1   **MAKE THE CHICKEN BROTH:** Place the chicken in a medium saucepan and add enough water to nearly submerge the chicken, so the breast isn't completely covered. Add the onion, garlic, and ginger and bring the water to a soft simmer over medium heat. Reduce the heat to medium-low and cook gently until the chicken is completely cooked through, 45 to 50 minutes. Turn off the heat and cool for 1 hour, then remove the chicken and strain the broth through a fine-mesh sieve into a medium bowl. Set aside (you can remove the chicken meat from the bones and save it to make the Chili-Honey Pulled Chicken below).

2   **MAKE THE CHICKEN IN THE POT:** Clean the same saucepan and add the Cornish hen to it, breast-side up. Add enough chicken broth to come halfway up the sides of the chicken. Bring the broth to a soft simmer over medium heat. Reduce the heat to medium-low and gently cook the chicken for 10 minutes. Turn the hen over for 5 minutes, then flip it breast-side up again for 10 minutes. Add the chayote, rice, garlic, ginger, salt, and pepper and continue to cook until the chayote is tender, 7 to 8 minutes.

3   Turn off the heat and transfer the hen to a cutting board. Cut the hen into pieces and divide them between two bowls. Divide the squash, aromatics, and broth between the bowls. Squeeze some lime juice over the top of each bowl and serve sprinkled with the scallions and cilantro.

VARIATION: CHILI-HONEY PULLED CHICKEN After poaching the chicken for the chicken broth, save the meat and toss it with the chili-orange glaze from the pork steak on page 88. Pile on a baguette with Holy Trinity (page 39) and you have a fantastic *num pang*.

beef-barley soup with bay and charred lemongrass

In Cambodia, beef was always a luxury, but when it was available, Ratha's mom made a soup like this one: brothy, rich, and jacked up with herbaceous lemongrass charred over charcoal to give it a smoky taste. The barley gets cooked separately from the soup until it is nearly al dente, then is added to the broth for the last few minutes of cooking. This is so the broth stays clear and doesn't get starchy.

1½ pounds beef chuck stew meat, cut into 1½-inch pieces

2 medium carrots, halved lengthwise, then thinly sliced crosswise

1 medium Yukon Gold potato, peeled and cut into ½-inch cubes

1 medium yellow onion, finely chopped

8 garlic cloves: 4 smashed and 4 finely chopped

6 fresh bay leaves, or 3 dried bay leaves

2 medium tomatoes, cored and cut into 1½-inch pieces

½ cup white wine

4 lemongrass stalks, ends trimmed

3 tablespoons canola oil

1 tablespoon plus 1 teaspoon kosher salt

2½ teaspoons sugar

1 (28-ounce) can crushed tomatoes

8 ounces mushrooms, stemmed, halved, and thinly sliced

2 celery stalks, thinly sliced crosswise

1 teaspoon freshly ground black pepper

¾ cup pearl barley, rinsed several times and drained

Finely chopped fresh Thai basil leaves, for serving

1 Place the stew meat in a large pot and add water to cover by 1½ inches. Bring the water to a boil over medium-high heat and skim off the impurities as they rise to the surface. Reduce the heat to medium-low and add the carrots, potato, half the onion, the smashed garlic, and the bay leaves. Simmer gently for 20 minutes, then add the fresh tomatoes and wine and simmer for 10 minutes more.

2 Char the lemongrass: Adjust an oven rack to the top position and preheat the broiler to high. Remove the tough outer layer of the lemongrass, then use the back spine of a chef's knife to smash it. Bend the dark green top over the reed and wrap it around, tying it around the stalk to secure it. Set the lemongrass on a baking sheet and broil for a few minutes until charred on both sides (watch the lemongrass closely as broiler intensities vary). Set aside.

3 In a large skillet, heat the oil over medium-high heat until it shimmers, about 2 minutes. Add the remaining onion, reduce the heat to medium, and cook, stirring often, until the onion starts to soften and become transparent, 3 to 4 minutes. Stir in the chopped garlic, 1 teaspoon of the salt, and ½ teaspoon of the sugar and cook until the garlic is fragrant, about 1 minute. Add the crushed tomatoes, reduce the heat to medium-low, and cook, stirring occasionally, until the oil pools on the surface of the tomatoes, 15 to 20 minutes. Turn off the heat, taste, and adjust with more salt, if needed. Add the mushrooms, celery, remaining 2 teaspoons sugar, 1 tablespoon salt, and the pepper. Cook for 50 minutes.

4   While the stew simmers, make the barley: Put the barley in a small saucepan and add cold water to cover by 1 inch. Bring the water to a simmer over medium-high heat. Reduce the heat to medium and cook until the barley is a little underdone and still quite chewy at the center, about 30 minutes. Drain, rinse with cold water, and set aside.

---

5   Once the meat easily falls apart when pressed against the side of the pot, add the charred lemongrass, cook for 10 minutes, then add the barley and cook until it is completely tender, about 10 minutes more. Remove and discard the lemongrass and bay leaves. Divide the soup among individual bowls and serve sprinkled with Thai basil.

oxtail stew

People who love oxtails *love* oxtails. The meat has the most beautiful and intense beefy taste and succulent texture you can imagine. Oxtails need a long time to tenderize, but cooked right—which means low and slow, like most stew cuts—you'll be rewarded with every bite. The tomatillos in the stew give it a needed bump of acidity that cuts through the richness of the broth. Pickled bean sprouts on the side are a *must*, as they add a ton of character and texture to the meal. This is great with rice or with garlic bread for sopping up the broth.

2 tablespoons canola oil

5 pounds oxtails, cut into 2- to 2½-inch-thick pieces, rinsed and patted dry

1 tablespoon kosher salt

12 whole star anise

1 tablespoon whole black peppercorns

2 teaspoons whole coriander seeds

1 teaspoon sugar

1 medium yellow onion, finely chopped

8 garlic cloves

4 plum tomatoes, halved lengthwise

2 teaspoons fish sauce

½ teaspoon fermented shrimp paste (see The Num Pang Pantry, page 25)

4 ounces fresh wood ear mushrooms, large pieces sliced in half

8 tomatillos, husked, rinsed well, and cut into bite-size pieces

¼ pound okra, sliced ½ inch thick

½ cup chopped fresh Thai basil leaves

Pickled Bean Sprouts (page 138)

2 limes, cut into wedges

heads-up

The okra takes just a few minutes to cook, so if you plan on making the stew in advance, wait to add the okra to the pot until you reheat the stew before serving. Slimy okra is no one's friend.

1   In a large and wide heavy-bottomed pot, heat the oil over medium-high heat until it shimmers, about 2 minutes. Season the oxtails with the salt and add them to the pot. Brown on all sides, about 30 minutes, browning in batches if needed. Transfer the oxtails to a bowl and set aside; pour off and discard all but 2 tablespoons of the oil from the pot.

2   Add the star anise, peppercorns, coriander, and sugar and cook until the spices become fragrant, then stir in the onion and garlic and cook, stirring often, until the onion is golden-brown, about 6 minutes.

3   Return the oxtails to the pot and add enough water to cover the oxtails by 2 inches. Reduce the heat to low, cover the pot, and cook gently for 1 hour. Stir in the tomatoes and continue to cook, stirring occasionally, until the meat falls away from the bone, 2 to 2½ hours.

4   Use a spoon to skim off and discard the fat at the surface. Stir in the fish sauce and shrimp paste, then add the mushrooms and tomatillos and gently simmer until the tomatillos are tender, about 10 minutes. Stir in the okra and cook just until tender, 5 minutes. Taste and add salt or more fish sauce, if needed. Divide the stew among bowls, top with Thai basil and pickled bean sprouts, and serve with a lime wedge.

beef stew with pickled cabbage, carrots, and cilantro

We use daikon instead of celery in the mirepoix base (the classic French onion-carrot-celery trio) for this stew. In combination with onions, carrots, and fennel, it adds a mellow, tender bite that is more silky than starchy and definitely less heavy than potatoes. The flavor of a braise or stew comes not just from what you add to the pot, but from the browned bits at the bottom of the pot. That's why it's really important to brown the meat well and in batches so it has the surface area it needs to caramelize. Pile in too much at once and the meat will steam, so not only will you lose the browned goodness on the meat, but you miss out on the magic *fond* on the bottom of the pot where beefy, browned umami is born—meat aside, it's that *fond* that is the real star in any braise or stew.

3 pounds well-marbled beef stew meat, cut into 2-inch pieces and patted dry with paper towels

2 tablespoons plus 1½ teaspoons freshly ground black pepper

1 tablespoon kosher salt

3 tablespoons all-purpose flour

2 tablespoons canola oil

2 tablespoons ground fennel seeds

1 medium yellow onion, finely chopped

2 medium carrots, finely chopped

1 medium daikon, finely chopped (about 1 cup)

1 medium fennel bulb, cored and finely chopped, fronds chopped and reserved for serving

1½ tablespoons tomato paste

2 cups fruity red wine (such as a Grenache or Malbec)

3 cups beef stock or broth

1   Season the beef with 1½ teaspoons of the pepper and the salt, then add the flour and lightly toss to combine. Heat a heavy-bottomed pot over high heat for 3 minutes, add the oil, and once you see a wisp of smoke rise from the pan, add about half the beef. Cook until the beef is browned on all sides, 8 to 10 minutes. Transfer the meat to a large bowl, pour off some of the fat in the pot (otherwise the meat will steam rather than brown) and add the remaining beef, browning it on all sides before transferring it to the bowl. Discard all but 2 tablespoons of the fat from the pot.

2   Add the remaining 2 tablespoons black pepper and the fennel seed to the pot and cook until fragrant, 15 to 30 seconds. Stir in the onion, carrots, daikon, fennel bulb, and tomato paste. Cook, stirring often, until the tomato paste is nicely browned, 3 to 4 minutes, then pour in the wine. Scrape up any browned bits from the bottom of the pan and simmer until the wine has reduced by three-quarters, about 8 minutes.

Steamed jasmine rice

½ bunch fresh cilantro, finely chopped

Holy Pickled Carrots (page 42)

Pickled Red Cabbage (page 142)

Store-bought fried onions (see The
  Num Pang Pantry, page 28)

4 scallions, thinly sliced on an angle

1 lime, cut into wedges

heads-up

You can serve the stew right away, but
the favors really do benefit from an
overnight rest in the fridge.

3   Return the beef to the pot and add enough stock to barely cover
    the beef. Reduce the heat to low and cover the pot with a piece
    of aluminum foil, crimping it around the edges to seal. Set a lid
    on the pot and cook very slowly until a fork meets no resistance
    sliding into the middle of a piece of meat, 1½ to 2 hours. Turn off
    the heat and let cool. Transfer the stew to an airtight container
    and refrigerate overnight (you can serve the stew now, but the
    flavors come together nicely if the stew has a chance to rest for a
    few hours).

4   Reheat the stew in a pot over medium-low heat. Serve over rice,
    garnished with the cilantro, reserved fennel fronds, pickled carrots,
    pickled cabbage, fried onions, the scallions, and a lime wedge.

KNOW THIS: USING SHALLOTS IN PLACE OF FRIED ONIONS OR GARLIC

With their quasi garlic-onion flavor, shallots are a decent substitute for store-bought crispy-fried onion or garlic (see The Num Pang Pantry, page 28). Deep-fried shallots offer the best flavor and crunch: Halve and thinly slice a shallot, then dredge it in flour and deep-fry it in a few inches of 350°F oil until crisp and browned. Use a slotted spoon or spider to transfer the fried shallots to a paper towel–lined plate to drain excess oil and immediately season with salt. Or, you can caramelize shallots in a skillet: Melt a couple tablespoons of butter, add the shallots, and cook over medium heat until the edges of the shallots become lightly browned. Reduce the heat to low and caramelize slowly until they get sticky sweet. Transfer the caramelized shallots to a paper towel–lined plate and season with salt. Salting at the end of cooking lets the shallot truly caramelize; if you add salt at the beginning of the cooking process, you'll draw out liquid and end up steaming them instead of caramelizing.

surf 'n' turf shepherd's pie

It's the shrimp cooked into the mashed potatoes that give this shepherd's pie its surf 'n' turf-ness. Shepherd's pie is usually loaded with peas and carrots, then topped with buttery mashed potatoes, but ours gets a Southeast Asian feel from turmeric and five-spice powder, as well as a few splashes of soy sauce. This is one of Ratha's son's favorite weeknight suppers.

MASHED POTATOES

2 pounds russet potatoes, peeled (leave the potatoes whole)

2½ teaspoons kosher salt

½ to ¾ cup whole milk

3 tablespoons (1½ ounces) unsalted butter

½ teaspoon garlic powder

1 cup peeled and deveined (21/30-count) shrimp (about 10 shrimp), halved crosswise

TURMERIC BEEF

3 tablespoons canola oil

1 small yellow onion, very finely chopped

1½ celery stalks, very finely chopped

1 small russet potato, peeled and very finely chopped

2 small garlic cloves, very finely chopped

1 teaspoon ground turmeric

½ teaspoon cayenne pepper

½ teaspoon dried oregano

½ teaspoon five-spice powder (see The Num Pang Pantry, page 28)

½ teaspoon sweet paprika

1½ teaspoons sugar

1½ teaspoons kosher salt

1¼ pounds 80% lean ground beef

1   **BOIL THE POTATOES FOR THE MASHED POTATOES:** Bring a large pot of water to a boil. Add the potatoes and 2 teaspoons of the salt and cook until a paring knife easily slips into the center of a potato, 20 to 25 minutes. Drain and set aside.

2   **MEANWHILE, MAKE THE TURMERIC BEEF:** In a large, deep skillet, heat 2 tablespoons of the oil over medium-high heat. Add the onion and stir occasionally until it starts to brown, 2 to 3 minutes. Stir in the celery, potato, and fresh garlic and cook, stirring occasionally, until the potato is tender and the onion is nicely browned, 7 to 8 minutes. Stir in the turmeric, cayenne, oregano, five-spice powder, paprika, ½ teaspoon of the sugar, and ½ teaspoon of the salt, then push the vegetables out to the edges of the skillet. Add the remaining 1 tablespoon oil to the center of the skillet and crumble in the beef (you don't want any large pieces). Once the beef starts to brown, 4 to 5 minutes, stir it into the vegetable mixture.

3   In a small bowl, stir together the soy sauce, remaining 1 teaspoon sugar, 1 teaspoon salt, and the black pepper. Add this to the beef mixture and cook until the meat starts to stick to the bottom of the skillet, about 5 minutes. Push the meat and vegetables out to the edges of the skillet and add the crushed tomatoes to the center, along with the garlic powder. Stir everything together and bring the beef mixture to a simmer. Add the chickpeas with their liquid and continue to cook until the flavors come together and the chickpeas soften, about 10 minutes.

3 tablespoons soy sauce

1 teaspoon freshly ground black pepper

1 (14-ounce) can crushed tomatoes

¼ teaspoon garlic powder

1 (14.5-ounce) can chickpeas, with their liquid

heads-up

The shrimp cooked into the mashed potatoes can be optional.

4   **FINISH THE MASHED POTATOES:** Return the drained potatoes to the saucepan and add ½ cup of the milk. Warm the potatoes in the milk over medium heat and start to smash them together, adding more milk if the mixture is too thick (you want a somewhat thin mash). Stir in the butter, garlic powder, and remaining ½ teaspoon salt, then add the shrimp. Reduce the heat to medium-low and cook until the shrimp are cooked through, 2 to 3 minutes. Serve a generous mound of the mashed potatoes with a big scoop of the turmeric beef on top.

KNOW THIS: WHAT MAKES IT CAMBODIAN?

A lot of people ask us how Cambodian food differs from, say, Vietnamese or Thai food. Cambodian food tends to be more rustic and hearty than both Vietnamese and Thai food, thanks to Cambodians' obsession with dried fish and shrimp and fermented shrimp and fish pastes like *prahok*. While aromatics like lemongrass, shallots, galangal, chiles, and garlic are commonalities among many Southeast Asian cuisines, in Cambodia cardamom, cloves, nutmeg, and turmeric, all spices considered to be more Indian than Southeast Asian, are traditional. The bright top notes from aromatics like fresh ginger and kaffir lime leaves combined with the depth from warm spices make Cambodian food totally different and unique from other cuisines of Southeast Asia. There are regional anomalies as well, and towns close to the Vietnam border, like where Ratha's paternal grandparents are from, are influenced by Vietnamese ingredients and traditions, while villages closer to Thailand might show more similarities to Thai food.

"clay pot" halibut

Halibut is one of the most prime types of fish you can buy. It's very rich and steak-y, with a succulence that makes it an excellent alternative to chops or chicken. In Cambodia, the fish (which is likely not as prime as halibut) gets cooked in a clay pot over fire; here in New York City, a burner and a skillet do the job just fine. This is essentially a more substantial version of the Peppercorn Catfish (page 111), that gets a stewlike quality from braised bok choy and daikon.

¾ cup soy sauce

⅓ cup honey

1 tablespoon sugar

3 teaspoons freshly ground black pepper

2 long and slender daikon, peeled, halved lengthwise, and cut crosswise into 2-inch pieces

2 tablespoons canola oil

2 (1½-pound) halibut steaks

1 teaspoon kosher salt

4 garlic cloves, lightly smashed

1 (1½-inch) piece fresh ginger, peeled and thinly sliced on an angle

1 head baby bok choy, separated from its base

Steamed rice (preferably jasmine), for serving

Thinly sliced scallions, for serving

1   In a small bowl, mix together the soy sauce, honey, sugar, and 1 teaspoon of the pepper and set aside.

2   Place the daikon in a medium saucepan and add water to cover. Cook over medium-high heat until the daikon are tender and the tip of a paring knife easily slips into one, about 20 minutes. Drain and set aside.

3   In a large, deep skillet (preferably nonstick), heat the oil over high heat. Season both sides of each halibut steak with the salt, then set them in the skillet and cook until nicely browned, about 4 minutes. Turn the halibut over and season with the remaining 2 teaspoons pepper. Crowd the fish together in the center of the skillet, reduce the heat to medium, and add the garlic and ginger around the edges of the pan. Cook, moving the garlic and ginger around occasionally (don't move the fish), until they are fragrant, 2 to 3 minutes.

4   Add the bok choy, the cooked daikon, and the soy sauce mixture and bring to a simmer, occasionally spooning the sauce over the top of the fish. Cook until the center part of the fish resists light pressure and is cooked through and the bok choy is tender, 3 to 4 minutes. Divide each halibut steak in half and serve with some of the daikon, bok choy, sauce, rice, and scallions.

cambodian mussels with tomatillos, okra, and garlic toast

Here you have some of the best flavors of the Southeast Asian table all together in one incredible bowl of food: fresh and peppery Thai basil, cilantro, briny mussels, and ginger-infused chicken broth. The real secrets to the amazingly robust and developed taste of the broth are dried shrimp and fermented shrimp paste. On their own, they smell like they could overpower your kitchen, let alone a bowl of mussels! But just a little bit of both gives the mussels a roundness and intensity that are totally unmatchable. You have to try this.

GARLIC TOAST

8 tablespoons (4 ounces) unsalted butter, at room temperature

2 garlic cloves, very finely chopped

1 (6-inch) length of baguette or 6-inch baguette, halved lengthwise

Kosher salt

MUSSELS

4 cups chicken broth (preferably homemade, see page 178)

2 tablespoons ground dried shrimp (see The Num Pang Pantry, page 25)

½ teaspoon fermented shrimp paste (see The Num Pang Pantry, page 25)

1 pound mussels, scrubbed and debearded

3 large okra, cut crosswise on a sharp angle into ¼-inch-thick pieces

2 tomatillos, husked, rinsed well, and cut into 1-inch-thick wedges

1 cup fresh bean sprouts

¼ teaspoon ground dried Thai bird's eye chile

2 tablespoons finely chopped fresh Thai basil leaves

2 tablespoons finely chopped fresh cilantro leaves, plus more for serving

1 lime, halved

1   **MAKE THE GARLIC TOAST:** Mix the butter and garlic together in a small bowl. Spread some butter over the cut sides of the bread. Sprinkle with salt and set aside.

2   **MAKE THE MUSSELS:** Bring the broth to a simmer in a large, deep skillet. Add the dried shrimp and the shrimp paste, reduce the heat to medium, and simmer for 1½ minutes. Add the mussels, okra, and tomatillos and cook until the mussels start to open, about 2 minutes. Use tongs to transfer the mussels to a large bowl; discard any that have not opened..

3   Stir the bean sprouts into the broth and continue to cook until the tomatillos are tender, about 3 minutes more. Stir in the chile, basil, and cilantro and squeeze in the juice from both lime halves. Return the mussels to the skillet and use a spoon to ladle the broth over the mussels. Turn off the heat.

recipe continues

Shrimp paste has a very strong odor. Only a small amount is used—it's what gives the broth its sharp salinity. Think of it as a shortcut instead of making shrimp stock.

4   Adjust an oven rack to the upper-middle position and heat the broiler to high. Place the bread on a rimmed baking sheet and toast until both sides are golden brown, 1 to 1½ minutes on each side. Set the bread on a cutting board and slice into 2-inch-wide pieces. Use a slotted spoon to divide the mussels among the bowls, discarding any that did not open. Add some broth and serve sprinkled with cilantro and with the garlic toast alongside.

KNOW THIS: FLAVOR SECRET IN A SHRIMP SHELL

You know that addictively delicious salty-savory-umami thing that happens in a lot of Southeast Asian food from phô broth to pad thai, congee to XO sauce? It leaves you feeling so . . . satiated. A lot of it starts with shrimp—not fresh shrimp, which is highly perishable, especially in the incredibly hot and humid regions of Cambodia, Vietnam, and Thailand, but dried and fermented shrimp. Both are available online or in Asian markets, both last a long, long time in the pantry or fridge, and both will totally transform your cooking. See The Num Pang Pantry on page 25 for more information about each.

loaded oatmeal

Breakfast is no excuse for blandness. Our bowl of steel-cut oats comes topped with candied ginger, mangoes, and papayas, toasted coconut, and highly addictive caramelized five-spiced cashews. Add the tangy-sweet tamarind–brown sugar syrup and there's no way you'll go back to a plain bowl of porridge again.

TAMARIND–BROWN SUGAR SYRUP

3 tablespoons tamarind concentrate
(see The Num Pang Pantry, page 35)

1 tablespoons packed dark brown sugar

Pinch of kosher salt

OATMEAL

1 cup steel-cut oats

¼ teaspoon kosher salt

½ cup unsweetened coconut flakes

2 tablespoons finely chopped
crystallized ginger

2 tablespoons finely chopped dried
mango

2 tablespoons finely chopped dried
papaya

½ cup coarsely chopped Five-Spice
Caramel Cashews (page 204)

heads-up

You can make a big pot of oats and keep them in the fridge. Oatmeal becomes firm and sliceable once chilled, so when you warm it up, add coconut milk, almond milk, or straight-up cow's milk (or water) to loosen the oats and make them good and creamy.

1   **MAKE THE TAMARIND–BROWN SUGAR SYRUP:** In a small bowl, mix the tamarind concentrate, brown sugar, salt, and 2 tablespoons cold water together. Set aside.

2   **MAKE THE OATMEAL:** Bring 4 cups water to a simmer in a medium saucepan over medium-high heat. While stirring with a wooden spoon, stream in the oats and add the salt. Reduce the heat to medium-low, set a lid on the saucepan so it is slightly askew, and simmer the oats gently until they are tender, 25 to 30 minutes.

3   Preheat the oven to 350°F. Spread the coconut on a rimmed baking sheet in an even layer and toast in the oven until golden, stirring midway through, 6 to 8 minutes. Transfer the coconut to a medium plate to cool.

4   Divide the oatmeal among four bowls, then sprinkle each with the coconut, crystallized ginger, dried mango and papaya, and some of the caramelized cashews. Drizzle with tamarind–brown sugar syrup and serve.

PART FIVE

in a bowl: cold

MAKE NO MISTAKE: Cambodia gets *hot* in the summertime. It's steamy, the air is heavy and thick, and it's swampy and humid beyond belief. Kind of like New York City! What feels good to eat is something refreshing, cooling, and invigorating, and that is what this chapter is all about: bright acidity, raw vegetables, and tons of herbs. The dishes here are generally quick to make and are immensely satisfying, whether you're eating them outside in the elements or in the luxury of an air-conditioned room.

cambodian slaw

In Cambodia, there's no real breakdown between the kinds of food you eat for breakfast, lunch, or dinner. A typical breakfast spread highlights a whole bunch of savory dishes, this fresh-and-fast slaw being one of them. It's an excellent summer dish since it's totally raw and requires no cooking (well, once the Tuk Trey Sauce on page 168 is made, that is). You can, of course, consolidate cabbages and use just one or two kinds, but we really like how the three intermix, with napa offering a frilly and delicate bite, savoy for crunch, and red cabbage making the slaw all that much more attractive.

4½ cups thinly sliced napa cabbage

¾ cup thinly sliced savoy cabbage

⅓ cup thinly sliced red cabbage

1 cup bean sprouts

½ red bell pepper, halved crosswise and thinly sliced

3 tablespoons coarsely chopped fresh Thai basil leaves

3 tablespoons coarsely chopped fresh cilantro leaves

1¼ cups Tuk Trey Sauce (page 168)

⅓ cup coarsely chopped salted roasted peanuts

¼ cup store-bought fried onions (see the Num Pang Pantry, page 28)

Toss the cabbages, sprouts, bell pepper, basil, and cilantro together in a large bowl. Drizzle with the Tuk Trey Sauce, then sprinkle the peanuts and fried onions over the top and serve.

VARIATION: TOFU SALAD Add 4 cups shredded romaine lettuce to the slaw. Whisk the Tuk Trey with ¼ cup canola oil and toss with the salad. Add 8 thinly sliced scallions. Serve Spicy Glazed Tofu (page 132) over the top.

VARIATION: NUM PANG NOODLE BOWL Take 1 part slaw and add 3 parts cooked rice noodles. Toss with ⅓ cup Tuk Trey, sprinkle with peanuts and fried onions, and serve.

green papaya salad

Eating this salad is like ingesting healthfulness—it's raw, crunchy, and incredibly vibrant. It wakes up your palate and is the best on a sticky, hot day. Papaya is loaded with healthy enzymes and vitamins and stuff, but we eat it because it just tastes so good.

6 medium dried shrimp (see The Num Pang Pantry, page 25)

1½ pounds unripe green papaya, peeled, halved lengthwise, and seeded

1 cup snow peas, thinly sliced lengthwise

1 small fresh Thai bird's eye chile, coarsely chopped

1 garlic clove, coarsely chopped

¼ cup plus 3 tablespoons palm sugar or lightly packed light brown sugar

Juice of 1½ limes

2 tablespoons fish sauce

1 pint cherry tomatoes, halved

⅓ cup coarsely chopped Spiced Peanuts (page 209), or roasted and salted peanuts

heads-up

A mandoline slicer fitted with the julienne attachment makes quick and easy work of slicing the papaya into uniformly thin strips, while a mortar and pestle creates the perfect texture and emulsion for the salad's tangy dressing. Use a large and wide mortar that can accommodate all the tomatoes. If you don't have a mortar and pestle, you can briefly pulse everything in a food processor—just take care not to overdo it.

1   Place the dried shrimp in a small bowl, cover with hot water, and set aside for 5 minutes. Drain the shrimp, then chop them crosswise into thirds.

2   Slice the papaya into thin pieces using a mandoline fitted with the julienne attachment, or using a chef's knife. Stack the slices, then slice again lengthwise into long, thin strips. (You should have about 5 cups sliced papaya.) Place the papaya in a large bowl and add the snow peas.

3   Using a mortar and pestle, pound the chile and garlic together into a rough paste. Add the shrimp and sugar and pound until blended, then add the lime juice and fish sauce, stirring the mixture until the sugar has dissolved. Add the tomatoes (work in batches, if necessary, depending on the size of your mortar) and crush them into the dressing.

4   Pour the dressing over the papaya and snow peas and toss to combine. Add the peanuts, toss again, and serve.

VARIATION: GREEN PAPAYA SALAD WITH SIZZLING PORK BELLY
Cut a few pieces of Glazed Five-Spice Pork Belly (page 78) into ½-inch cubes. Heat a medium skillet over medium-high heat. Add ½ tablespoon canola oil and the pork belly cubes and brown the pork cubes on all sides until caramelized, then sprinkle them over the salad and serve.

kale and apple salad

We don't think that there is a restaurant menu in NYC that hasn't be influenced by our kale-loving neighbors across the river in Brooklyn. A dish from a local Chinese takeout joint gave Ben the idea for our spin on the raw kale salad. To lighten the flavor of the greens, we dress them with a blended vinaigrette made with toasted sesame oil, sugar, fresh ginger, black sesame seeds, and a little pureed raw kale to give the dressing a pale green color. We sell out of this salad—at every location—every day.

1½ tablespoons black sesame seeds

4½ tablespoons canola oil

1 tablespoon toasted sesame oil

1½ tablespoons rice vinegar

1½ tablespoons soy sauce

1½ tablespoons sugar

½ teaspoon kosher salt

1 scallion, green part only, thinly sliced

Heaping 1 tablespoon coarsely chopped fresh ginger

1 bunch kale, stems removed, leaves stacked, rolled, and thinly sliced crosswise into ribbons

1 medium carrot, grated

1 apple, cored and chopped into ¼-inch pieces

1   Toast the sesame seeds in a small skillet over medium-low heat. Once they are fragrant, 1½ to 2 minutes, transfer 1 tablespoon to a blender.

2   To the blender, add, in this order, the canola oil, sesame oil, vinegar, soy sauce, sugar, salt, scallion, ginger, and one-quarter of the kale. Blend on high speed until the vinaigrette is semismooth and emulsified, about 30 seconds.

3   Put the remaining kale in a salad bowl and add the carrot and apple. Add the vinaigrette and use your hands to toss the salad until all the leaves are well coated. Serve with the remaining sesame seeds sprinkled over the top.

tomato-watermelon salad

Simple and refreshing, we love the summer day when this salad makes its annual debut on our menu. It's sweet and spicy, a little savory, and has the right tang and fresh, herby flavor, making it great on its own or as a side dish to any summery protein. Could you add a couple of other ingredients to the salad? Sure. Does it need it? Absolutely not.

1 seedless baby watermelon, or 8 cups 1-inch watermelon cubes

2 to 3 large tomatoes, cored and cut into 1-inch cubes (about 4 cups)

1 cup small fresh Thai basil leaves (leave whole)

3 large pinches of ground dried Thai bird's eye chile or cayenne pepper

¼ cup extra-virgin olive oil

1½ tablespoons apple cider vinegar

¾ teaspoon kosher salt

1   Set the watermelon on a cutting board and slice off the ends to expose the pink fruit. Stand the watermelon upright and slice off the rind from top to bottom, following the curve of the melon to stay as close to the pink fruit as possible. Chop the melon into 1-inch cubes and place them in a large bowl (you should have about 8 cups).

2   Add the tomatoes, basil, chile, oil, vinegar, and salt and use your hands to gently toss the salad to combine. Cover the bowl with plastic wrap and refrigerate for 15 minutes, then serve.

KNOW THIS: TREAT YOUR BASIL GENTLY

Basil will blacken once it's cut, which is why we like to use tiny whole Thai basil leaves in salads or other dishes where seeing the whole, perfect leaf makes a difference. If you don't have enough small leaves to yield what the recipe calls for, stack some larger leaves and run your knife through them just once to halve them. Don't rock the knife back and forth or you'll bruise the leaves.

grilled fig and five-spice caramel cashew salad

Spicing nuts is a great way to add an exotic note to a dish. We take ours a step further by caramelizing the cashews in melted sugar before spicing them—the hot sugar syrup toasts the nuts and gives them an extra hit of sweetness and crunch. You could use peanuts or even walnuts here. Make a big batch and you'll catch yourself tossing them into everything, from salads to oatmeal (page 195) and even pasta. They're *that* good and *that* versatile. Don't say we didn't warn you . . .

FIVE-SPICE CARAMEL CASHEWS

½ cup sugar

4 tablespoons (2 ounces) unsalted butter, at room temperature

¼ cup five-spice powder (see The Num Pang Pantry, page 28)

1½ cups roasted salted cashews

SALAD

4 tablespoons canola oil

2 tablespoons rice vinegar

1 tablespoon toasted sesame oil

1 tablespoon grated peeled fresh ginger

4 scallions, green parts only, thinly sliced

¾ teaspoon kosher salt

½ teaspoon ground black pepper

12 fresh black figs, halved

3 heads Bibb lettuce, leaves separated and roughly torn

heads-up

If you burn caramel, it's nothing to fear. Simply add some water to the pan and bring it to a boil. The hot water will melt the rocklike sugar, meaning you can clean the pan (without a chisel). Do take care when caramelizing sugar: have an oven mitt at the ready—the last thing you want is to get the molten sugar syrup on your skin . . . ouch!

1   **MAKE THE FIVE-SPICE CARAMEL CASHEWS:** Line a rimmed baking sheet with parchment paper. Set a medium skillet over medium heat and add the sugar to the pan, shaking it into an even layer. Melt the sugar, shaking the pan occasionally, until it is melted and golden, 8 to 10 minutes (take care as you swirl or shake the pan—the sugar is very, very hot!). Continue to cook the sugar until it is golden brown, shaking and swirling the pan as needed, to get the sugar to caramelize evenly. Add the butter and whisk it in as it melts, then whisk in the five-spice powder. Quickly add the cashews, stirring them to coat in the caramel. Immediately turn the nuts out onto the prepared baking sheet and set aside.

2   **MAKE THE SALAD:** In a blender, combine 3 tablespoons of the canola oil, the vinegar, sesame oil, ginger, scallions, ½ teaspoon of the salt, and ¼ teaspoon of the pepper and pulse until semismooth (you don't want a totally smooth and emulsified dressing; it should be a little rough textured).

3   Heat a charcoal or gas grill to medium, or heat a grill pan over medium heat. Put the figs in a medium bowl and toss with the remaining 1 tablespoon canola oil, ¼ teaspoon salt, and ¼ teaspoon pepper. Set the figs on the grill and cook on both sides until grill marked, 3 to 4 minutes total. Transfer to a plate and set aside.

4   Place the lettuce leaves in a large bowl and toss with enough dressing to lightly coat the leaves. Turn the dressed lettuce onto a large platter, then break up the cashews and sprinkle them over the top. Add the grilled figs, drizzle them with a little dressing, and serve.

roasted beet salad with pickled shallots

Beets take a little extra time to roast, peel, and chill, but they're so nutritious and flavorful that we feel the extra work pays off. We roast beets in a baking dish with water and covered with aluminum foil. The water helps to steam the beets, keep them moist, prevent them from sticking and the sugars from turning bitter, and also makes rubbing the skin off (we use a paper towel) incredibly quick and easy. Save some time by hunting down vacuum-sealed preroasted beets. Most supermarkets stock them in the produce department, usually near the tofu.

6 medium beets, scrubbed well

2 tablespoons whole coriander seeds

1¼ cups apple cider vinegar

3 tablespoons sugar

1 tablespoon kosher salt

1 dried Thai bird's eye chile

4 medium shallots, very thinly sliced into rings (preferably using a mandoline)

½ cup extra-virgin olive oil

½ teaspoon freshly ground black pepper

½ lemon, for serving

¼ cup roasted salted peanuts or cashews, for serving

1 cup fresh cilantro leaves

Flaky sea salt, for serving

1   Preheat the oven to 375°F. Place the beets in a baking dish and add 1 tablespoon of the coriander seeds and 1½ cups water. Cover the baking dish with aluminum foil and roast until a fork slips into the center of the largest beet with no resistance, about 1 hour. Remove the baking dish from the oven, uncover, and set aside until the beets are cool enough to handle (but still slightly warm), about 20 minutes. Using a paper towel, rub off the skins from the beets (this will be messy—gloves help) and chop the beets into 1½-inch pieces.

2   While the beets roast, pickle the shallots: In a medium saucepan, combine 1 cup of the vinegar, the sugar, salt, chile, and 1 cup water. Bring the liquid to a simmer over medium-high heat, add the shallots, turn off the heat, and set aside to cool for 1 hour. Remove and discard the chile and strain the shallots, discarding the pickling liquid.

3   In a small skillet, toast the remaining 1 tablespoon coriander seeds over medium heat until golden brown and fragrant, shaking the pan often, 1 to 2 minutes. Turn off the heat and transfer the coriander to a medium plate to cool, then grind it in a spice grinder or using a mortar and pestle.

4   In a large bowl, combine the pickled shallots, oil, remaining ¼ cup vinegar, ground toasted coriander, pepper, and beets. Toss to combine and refrigerate for 30 minutes until chilled. Squeeze the lemon over the salad, then serve sprinkled with the peanuts, cilantro, and sea salt.

greenmarket gazpacho

During our first summer at Num Pang on University Place and 12th Street, all we had to do to be inspired was venture out two short blocks to the Union Square Greenmarket for edible inspiration. Stalls upon stalls are brimming with finds every season, but late spring into late fall is really where it's at. This gazpacho gets an Asian feel from cilantro, Thai basil, and a splash of rice vinegar, but aside from those additions, it's a fairly classic take on a summer standby.

5 medium Kirby cucumbers, unpeeled, sliced crosswise into thick rounds

4 cups tomato juice, plus more as needed

1¼ cups fresh cilantro leaves

2 red bell peppers, seeded and quartered

1 jalapeño, halved lengthwise (remove the seeds from all or half the jalapeño for less heat)

5 ripe medium tomatoes, cored and quartered

1 cup fresh Thai basil leaves

2 teaspoons kosher salt, plus more as needed

½ teaspoon freshly ground black pepper, plus more as needed

2 to 3 tablespoons rice vinegar, plus more as needed

1 In a blender, combine half the cucumbers, half the cilantro, half the bell peppers, half the jalapeño, half the tomatoes, half the basil, the salt, black pepper, 2 cups of the tomato juice, and the vinegar. Blend until the mixture is mostly smooth, with some chunkier bits in the mix. Pour the gazpacho into a large container.

2 Add the remaining cucumbers, cilantro, bell peppers, jalapeño, tomatoes, basil, and tomato juice to the blender. Process the mixture until it is the consistency you want—less for a chunky gazpacho and more for a smooth gazpacho. Add it to the first batch and taste. Adjust the flavor with more tomato juice (if the gazpacho is too thick), salt, pepper, or vinegar, if needed. Refrigerate the gazpacho until it is very cold, at least 1 hour or up to a few days. Serve cold.

heads-up

Save some of the gazpacho to use as a base for a really good Bloody Mary. Thin it with extra tomato juice and plenty of vodka (or tequila, for a Bloody Maria).

glass noodle salad with spiced peanuts

Anyone who says cold pasta salad is boring has yet to try this one. Glass noodles made from mung bean sprouts become clear after soaking (they're often called cellophane noodles) and have a springy, bouncy bite that makes them fun to eat. Tossed with crunchy vegetables, our five-spice peanut brittle, and loads of fresh herbs, this salad will totally get you to rethink the "pasta salad" genre.

SPICED PEANUTS

Nonstick spray

½ cup granulated sugar

4 tablespoons (2 ounces) unsalted butter, at room temperature

¼ cup five-spice powder (see The Num Pang Pantry, page 28)

1½ cups roasted salted peanuts

NOODLE SALAD

5 ounces mung bean vermicelli noodles

1 teaspoon kosher salt

Heaping ¼ cup snow peas

¼ cup soy sauce

1½ tablespoons lightly packed light brown sugar

1 tablespoon toasted sesame oil

4 scallions, green parts only, thinly sliced

¼ medium red bell pepper, very thinly sliced lengthwise

¼ cup fresh cilantro leaves

¼ cup fresh Thai basil leaves

1 tablespoon black sesame seeds, toasted

heads-up

The dressed noodles need 1 hour to chill in the fridge. This allows the flavors to really mesh. Of course roasted, salted peanuts can stand in for the five-spice caramel nuts, but c'mon . . . do you really want them to?

1 **MAKE THE SPICED PEANUTS:** Lightly coat a rimmed baking sheet with nonstick spray. Set a medium skillet over medium heat and add the sugar to the pan, shaking it into an even layer. Melt the sugar, shaking the pan occasionally, until the sugar is melted and golden, 8 to 10 minutes (take care as you swirl or shake the pan—the sugar is very, very hot!). Continue to cook the sugar until it is golden brown, shaking and swirling the pan as needed, to get the sugar to caramelize evenly. Whisk in the butter, then whisk in the five-spice powder. Quickly stir in the peanuts and immediately turn the nuts out onto the prepared baking sheet. Set aside to cool, then coarsely chop the brittle.

2 **MAKE THE NOODLE SALAD:** Put the noodles in a large heat-safe bowl, cover with cold water, and set aside for 15 minutes. Bring a saucepan of water to a boil. Drain the noodles, return them to the bowl, and cover with the boiling water. Soak until tender, about 3 minutes, drain, and cool completely.

3 Fill a bowl with ice and water and set aside. Bring a small saucepan of water to a boil over high heat. Add the salt and snow peas and cook until they are bright green, 45 seconds to 1 minute. Drain and plunge into the ice water. Blot dry and thinly slice lengthwise.

4 In a large bowl, whisk together the soy sauce, brown sugar, and oil until the sugar has dissolved. Add the drained noodles, the scallions, bell peppers, blanched snow peas, cilantro, and basil and toss to combine. Cover the bowl with plastic wrap and refrigerate for 1 hour.

5 To serve, toss the salad, divide among bowls, and sprinkle with the crushed spiced peanuts and the sesame seeds.

cambodian ceviche

Fish is a major player in Cambodian cuisine, so having a cold yet fiery-tasting ceviche makes a lot of sense. There are lots of components to this seemingly simple dish, but they all come together in a beautiful and sophisticated way. While the calamari gets quickly pan-seared, the shrimp gets "cooked" in the lime juice. Once the squid is chilled, it is tossed in the spicy-lime marinade. Be sure to buy whatever sushi-grade fish your fishmonger has available, and make sure it looks vibrant, has a nice sheen, and smells fresh and clean. Fluke is a nice choice because it has a very mellow flavor and serves as a nice canvas for the other ingredients in the ceviche. If fluke isn't available, go for other medium-firm and mild options like red snapper or grouper.

1 medium sweet potato, peeled and cut into ½-inch cubes

2 tablespoons canola oil

1 teaspoon kosher salt, plus a pinch

½ teaspoon freshly ground black pepper

8 ounces calamari rings and tentacles

2 limes

1 teaspoon minced red onion

1 garlic clove, very finely chopped

1 small jalapeño, very finely chopped

1 teaspoon sugar

Few pinches of ground dried Thai bird's eye chile

8 ounces rock shrimp or bay scallops

8 ounces sushi-grade fluke, very thinly sliced crosswise

¼ large Asian pear, peeled, cored, and cut into ½-inch cubes

4 large fresh Thai basil leaves, thinly sliced

1   Preheat the oven to 375°F. Place the sweet potato on a rimmed baking sheet and toss with 1 tablespoon of the oil, ½ teaspoon of the salt, and ¼ teaspoon of the pepper. Place the sweet potato in the oven and roast until tender, about 25 minutes. Remove from the oven and let cool to room temperature on the baking sheet. Transfer the sweet potato to a large plate, then refrigerate to chill thoroughly.

2   In a medium skillet, heat the remaining 1 tablespoon oil over medium heat. Add the calamari and a pinch of salt and cook, stirring often, until the calamari is cooked through, 3 to 4 minutes. Transfer the calamari to a medium plate and refrigerate until well chilled.

3   Juice 1½ limes into a large bowl and quarter the remaining lime half; set the lime quarters aside. Add the onion, garlic, jalapeño, sugar, the remaining salt and pepper, and the ground chile to the bowl with the lime juice and whisk to combine. Add the shrimp and toss to combine.

4   Divide the fluke among four plates. Add the chilled calamari, sweet potatoes, Asian pear, and basil to the bowl with the shrimp and mix well. Top the fluke with the shrimp ceviche mixture. Divide any remaining liquid from the bowl over each plate and serve with a lime wedge.

garlic chive oil

Blanching the garlic chives and shocking them in ice water before blending ensures that their color remains bright and vibrant. We use this oil to make the Garlic Chive Vinaigrette (page 213), but it's also beautiful drizzled over soup, a piece of grilled chicken, or added to roasted vegetables. If you can't find garlic chives (we get them from Asian markets) use regular chives.

1 tablespoon kosher salt, plus more as needed

1 cup fresh garlic chives (see The Num Pang Pantry, page 28) or regular chives

1 medium garlic clove, finely chopped (only if using regular chives)

1 to 1¼ cups canola oil

Pinch of kosher salt (optional)

1   Fill a bowl with ice and water and set aside. Bring a small saucepan of water to a boil and add the salt. Add the garlic chives, and once they wilt after a second or two, use a slotted spoon to transfer them to the ice water bath to cool. Once cool, transfer them to a paper towel and squeeze all the water out, effectively pressing them into a tight ball. Set the chive ball on a cutting board and run a sharp knife through it once.

2   Place the chives in a blender. If using regular chives, add the garlic. Add enough oil to cover the chives by 1 inch (you may not need all the oil). Blend in quick pulses, scraping down the sides of the blender jar as needed; don't let the blender run too long or the oil will get hot and turn brown.

3   Taste the chive oil and add a pinch of salt if needed. Transfer to an airtight container and refrigerate for up to 5 days.

VARIATION: THAI BASIL OIL Substitute Thai basil (see The Num Pang Pantry, page 35) for the chives (don't use the garlic). Blanch and blend as instructed.

garlic chive vinaigrette

We like the garlicky quality that the Garlic Chive Oil (page 212) lends this vinaigrette. It's especially good tossed with salad or slaw (page 198). It's also nice as a marinade for chicken breasts and fish. While the Garlic Chive Oil keeps for up to five days, the vinaigrette only stays fresh tasting for up to one day—after that, the lime loses its edge, so try to use the vinaigrette within one day of making it.

Juice of 2 limes (3 to 4 tablespoons)
½ teaspoon kosher salt, plus more as needed
¼ teaspoon freshly ground black pepper, plus more as needed
1½ cups Garlic Chive Oil (page 212)

In a medium bowl, whisk together the lime juice, salt, and pepper. Slowly drizzle in the garlic chive oil while whisking continuously to create a creamy emulsion. Taste and adjust the salt and pepper if needed. Refrigerate and shake to reemulsify before using.

VARIATION: THAI BASIL VINAIGRETTE Substitute Thai Basil Oil (page 212) for the Garlic Chive Oil.

PART SIX

to drink

JUST LIKE WITH OUR FOOD, when it comes to drinks, we go for flavor-forward concoctions. Ginger, tamarind, coconut milk, lime, tea, honey . . . many of these additions complement our teas and fruit juice blends. The goal is for the drink to offer a refreshing blast after a few bites of food—whether the drink is served warm or cold, it's about quenching your thirst and adding another layer to the experience of eating at Num Pang.

jasmine iced tea

Simple syrup is a liquid sweetener generally made with equal parts sugar and water, but we like adding honey to the mix to add its natural sweetness. It rounds out the flavor of this iced green jasmine–scented tea nicely (we also use it in the Ginger-Pineapple Iced Tea on page 217 and the Blood Orange Lemonade on page 219). Plain ice cubes have a tendency to dilute a drink when they melt—avoid this entirely by freezing tea, coffee, or even lemonade in an ice cube tray, then use the flavored cubes to chill the drink.

HONEY SIMPLE SYRUP

½ cup sugar

½ cup honey

JASMINE TEA

1 cup loose-leaf green jasmine tea

Lots of ice cubes

heads-up

The Honey Simple Syrup keeps in the fridge for up to 2 weeks.

1   **MAKE THE HONEY SIMPLE SYRUP:** Combine the sugar and honey to a small saucepan, then pour in 1 cup water. Bring the mixture to a boil, stirring occasionally to dissolve the sugar, then turn off the heat, set aside to cool, and refrigerate until chilled.

2   **MAKE THE JASMINE TEA:** In a medium saucepan, bring 10 cups water to a simmer over medium-high heat. Place the tea in a large teapot or heat-safe bowl, add the simmering water, cover, and set aside to steep for 3 minutes. Pour the tea through a fine-mesh sieve into a large pitcher or glass jug. Set aside to cool, then refrigerate until thoroughly chilled.

3   Fill a glass with ice and add some chilled tea. Top off with honey simple syrup to taste and serve.

KNOW THIS: JASMINE TEA

Jasmine tea is made by infusing jasmine blossoms into dry tea over a period of time, with the higher-quality teas being very gently infused with jasmine blossoms more than a half dozen times. Green tea is most often used as the tea base for jasmine tea, and it's what we use in our stores. Jasmine tea has this incredible floral taste that is balanced by the tannins and bitterness of the green tea. We soften and sweeten the tea's edge with Honey Simple Syrup, but even a squeeze of honey or a spoonful of sugar gets the job done. Buying loose-leaf tea is the least expensive option—plus, you usually get a better quality than what is portioned into tea bags. The tea comes in blooming "flowers" and little marble-size balls, but we just go classic with the dried, loose leaves.

ginger-pineapple iced tea

Tropical fruits are big all over Cambodia—pineapple, mango, lychee. They're all refreshing antidotes to a steamy day, or even a chilly one when you just need a flash of something fresh and exciting in your mouth. This iced tea gets heat and spice from the ginger and a sweet-sour tropical roundness from the pineapple. The Honey Simple Syrup gives it an extra layer of warmth and natural sweetness.

GINGER-PINEAPPLE SIMPLE SYRUP

1¼ cups Honey Simple Syrup (page 216)

½ cup 1-inch pieces fresh pineapple

¼ cup coarsely chopped peeled fresh ginger

¼ teaspoon kosher salt

JASMINE TEA

1 cup loose-leaf green jasmine tea

Lots of ice cubes

heads-up

The Ginger-Pineapple Simple Syrup keeps in the fridge for about 1 week.

1   **MAKE THE GINGER-PINEAPPLE SIMPLE SYRUP:** In a blender, combine the honey simple syrup, pineapple, ginger, and salt and puree until totally smooth. Pour the syrup through a fine-mesh sieve into a medium bowl and set aside to cool, then refrigerate to chill.

2   **MAKE THE JASMINE TEA:** In a medium saucepan, bring 10 cups water to a simmer over medium-high heat. Place the tea in a large teapot or heat-safe bowl, add the simmering water, cover, and set aside to steep for 3 minutes. Pour the tea through a fine-mesh sieve into a large pitcher or glass jug. Set aside to cool, then refrigerate until thoroughly chilled.

3   Fill a glass with ice and add 1¼ cups of the chilled tea. Top off with some of the ginger-pineapple simple syrup and serve.

blood orange lemonade

The slightly bitter flavor of blood orange is a natural companion to honey-sweetened lemonade. The combination is sophisticated and great for anyone who likes a soft bitterness to their fruit juices. We tend to make our juices on the tart side, so if you want it sweeter, add more Honey Simple Syrup.

2 cups fresh lemon juice
(from 8 to 10 lemons)

2 cups blood orange juice
(from 4 to 5 blood oranges)

1¼ cups Honey Simple Syrup
(page 216)

Pinch of kosher salt

Ice, for serving

In a large pitcher, combine the lemon juice, blood orange juice, simple syrup, salt, and 2 cups cold water. Stir to combine and serve over ice.

heads-up

Blood oranges are only in season for a few months in the late winter. If you can't find fresh oranges to juice, buy bottled blood orange juice. It's not the same, but pretty good nonetheless.

watermelon juice

What makes our watermelon juice so satisfying? A four-letter secret called salt (we add salt to our Blood Orange Lemonade, page 219, and Ginger-Pineapple Iced Tea, page 217, too). The salt gives the juice an underlying savory quality that is totally thirst-quenching on a steamy summer city day. This recipe easily doubles or triples; you'll just have to blend it with the salt in batches.

1 seedless baby watermelon, or 8 cups
   1-inch watermelon cubes
1 teaspoon kosher salt

1   Set the watermelon on a cutting board and slice off the ends to expose the pink fruit. Stand the watermelon upright and slice off the rind from top to bottom, following the curve of the melon to stay as close to the pink fruit as possible. Chop the melon into 1-inch cubes and place them in a large bowl (you should have about 8 cups).

2   Blend the watermelon with the salt. Transfer to an airtight container and refrigerate to chill completely before serving.

heads-up

Always taste the watermelon before blending it. If your melon isn't sweet enough, add a glug or two of Honey Simple Syrup (page 216) to the blender.

berry punch

Berries were a revelation to Ratha when he moved to America from Cambodia, where he had never seen a strawberry, raspberry, or blueberry, let alone tasted one. After his first berry experience, he was totally blown away, and to this day, when berries are in season, he can't get enough of them. This drink celebrates all the sweet juiciness of ripe summer berries that flood the farmers' markets in New York City in midsummer. You can make the punch with any combination of berries, even frozen ones if you can't find sweet, fresh ones. A little ginger ale adds a bit of fizz that perks up the whole combination.

4 cups fresh or frozen blueberries

2 cups apple juice

2 cups fresh or frozen raspberries

¼ cup orange juice (preferably freshly squeezed)

Pinch of kosher salt

Ice, for serving

1 can ginger ale

1   In a blender, combine the blueberries, apple juice, raspberries, orange juice, and salt and puree until smooth.

2   Fill four glasses with ice and divide the berry juice among the glasses. Top off with ginger ale.

heads-up

This punch is great served spiked with cava or sparkling wine.

cambodian iced coffee

Buying a young coconut from a street hawker was a huge part of growing up in Cambodia. Ratha used to cut the top off and drink the coconut water straight from the coconut, then use a spoon to scoop out the tender flesh inside. He tapped into that experience for our iced coffee, which gets depth from coconut milk and a sweet-sour-bitter note from tamarind. The condensed milk adds body and richness, and is a play on beloved Vietnamese iced coffee.

COCONUT-TAMARIND CONDENSED MILK

1½ cups sweetened condensed milk (about one and a quarter 14-ounce cans)

¾ cup plus 2 tablespoons coconut milk

1 tablespoons liquid tamarind concentrate (see The Num Pang Pantry, page 35)

¾ teaspoon kosher salt

Ice, for serving

4 cups strong brewed coffee, chilled

1 **MAKE THE COCONUT-TAMARIND CONDENSED MILK:** In a small skillet, combine the condensed milk, coconut milk, tamarind concentrate, and salt and heat over medium-low heat. Begin to reduce the mixture, whisking often over very gentle heat, until the mixture thickens and has reduced to about 2 cups, about 30 minutes. (Note that after 5 to 10 minutes, the mixture will thicken quite suddenly—don't worry, just keep whisking so that it doesn't burn at the bottom of the saucepan.)

2 Add ice to four glasses and divide the coffee among the glasses. Top with the coconut-tamarind condensed milk and serve.

heads-up

In our shops, we use ⅓ cup of the condensed milk mixture to sweeten 1 cup of coffee. Adjust the amount of coconut-tamarind condensed milk to suit your sweet tooth (ours is pretty long).

warm ginger-apple cider

––––––

In our original 12th Street location, we didn't have the space to brew coffee, but we wanted to offer our customers something warm to drink during the frigid wintertime. Since we already had apple cider in the kitchen (we use it in marinades, for braising, and for sauces) it made sense to offer it warm in a cup. But of course we had to give it a Num Pang spin, so we added loads of fresh ginger to give it a chest-warming quality. If you feel a chill coming on, a cup of this will set you right.

12 cups apple cider

¼ cup finely chopped peeled fresh ginger

2 tablespoons honey

2¼ teaspoons sugar

¾ teaspoon kosher salt

1 In a large saucepan, combine the apple cider, ginger, honey, sugar, and salt and bring to a simmer over medium-high heat.

2 Reduce the heat to low and gently cook until the cider is very fragrant, about 30 minutes. Serve warm.

heads-up

Spike the hot cider with a shot of whiskey, bourbon, or Scotch.

give more

As restaurateurs and members of the food community, we believe in supporting organizations that work to create better lives for those who need help. Here are just a few charities that we have supported as a company and also through our Guest Chefs program (see page 59). They all benefit worthy causes and would be grateful to have your support, be it through a monetary contribution or a donation of your time and expertise.

BROOKLYN ANIMAL RESOURCE COALITION

barcshelter.org

CAMBODIAN CHILDREN'S FUND

cambodianchildrensfund.org

DOUBLE H RANCH

doublehranch.org

EDIBLE SCHOOLYARD NYC

esynyc.org

FOOD BANK FOR NEW YORK CITY

foodbanknyc.org

GOD'S LOVE WE DELIVER

glwd.org

NORTH SHORE ANIMAL LEAGUE

animalleague.org

TUESDAY'S CHILDREN

tuesdayschildren.org

THE YOUNG SCIENTIST FOUNDATION

theyoungscientistfoundation.org

index

NOTE: Page references in *italics* indicate photographs.

author bios

RATHA CHAUPOLY AND BEN DAITZ met on the Clark University campus in 1992. When they reconnected in New York City in 1998, they were surprised to discover that they were both working in the restaurant industry. After learning about their shared love of the culinary world, the pair decided to open the Num Pang Sandwich Shop near Union Square in March of 2009, and a location in Midtown East soon after. With graffiti art on the walls and '80s/'90s hip-hop blasting from the speakers, the shops attracted crowds who lined up all the way down the block to order the creative Asian sandwiches and sides that combine the flavors from Ratha's childhood in Cambodia with Ben's culinary technique. Num Pang has consistently been rated the best sandwich shop in New York City by Zagat and has drawn accolades from publications such as *Bon Appétit*, *The Village Voice*, and more. There are eight Num Pang locations in NYC, including a flagship in the NoMad neighborhood, Brookfield Place, Chelsea Market, and Times Square, with more on the way.

RAQUEL PELZEL is an award-winning food writer and cookbook author. She has coauthored more than a dozen cookbooks including her own cookbook, *Toast*, and was an editor at *Cook's Illustrated* and the senior food editor for Tasting Table. She lives in Brooklyn.